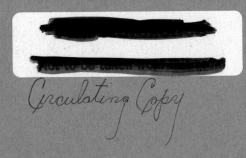

Volume VII

TIME
LIFE
BOOKS
®

Other Publications:
UNDERSTANDING COMPUTERS
YOUR HOME
THE ENCHANTED WORLD
THE KODAK LIBRARY OF CREATIVE PHOTOGRAPHY
GREAT MEALS IN MINUTES
THE CIVIL WAR
PLANET EARTH
COLLECTOR'S LIBRARY OF THE CIVIL WAR
THE EPIC OF FLIGHT
THE GOOD COOK
THE SEAFARERS
WORLD WAR II
HOME REPAIR AND IMPROVEMENT
THE OLD WEST

For information on and a full description of any of the Time-Life Books series listed above, please write:
Reader Information
Time-Life Books
641 North Fairbanks Court
Chicago, Illinois 60611

This volume is one of a series
that chronicles American culture from 1870 to 1970.

This Fabulous Century

1960
1970

Volume VII

By the Editors of TIME-LIFE BOOKS

Time-Life Books, Alexandria, Virginia

Time-Life Books Inc.
is a wholly owned subsidiary of
TIME INCORPORATED

FOUNDER: Henry R. Luce 1898-1967

Editor-in-Chief: Henry Anatole Grunwald
President: J. Richard Munro
Chairman of the Board: Ralph P. Davidson
Corporate Editor: Jason McManus
Group Vice President, Books: Reginald K. Brack Jr.
Vice President, Books: George Artandi

TIME-LIFE BOOKS INC.

EDITOR: George Constable
Executive Editor: George Daniels
Editorial General Manager: Neal Goff
Director of Design: Louis Klein
Editorial Board: Dale M. Brown, Roberta Conlan,
Ellen Phillips, Gerry Schremp, Gerald Simons,
Rosalind Stubenberg, Kit van Tulleken, Henry Woodhead
Director of Research: Phyllis K. Wise
Director of Photography: John Conrad Weiser

PRESIDENT: William J. Henry
Senior Vice President: Christopher T. Linen
Vice Presidents: Stephen L. Bair, Robert A. Ellis,
John M. Fahey Jr., Juanita T. James, James L. Mercer,
Joanne A. Pello, Paul R. Stewart, Christian Strasser

THIS FABULOUS CENTURY

EDITOR: Ezra Bowen
Editorial Staff for *Volume VII, 1960-1970*
Picture Editor: Carlotta Kerwin
Designer: Charles Mikolaycak
Assistant Designer: Jean Lindsay Morein
Staff Writers: George Constable, Betsy Frankel,
Lee Greene, Sam Halper, Anne Horan, Lucille Schulberg,
Suzanne Seixas, Bryce S. Walker
Researchers: Alice Baker, Terry Drucker,
Helen Greenway, Helen M. Hinkle, Carol Isenberg,
Nancy J. Jacobsen, Myra Mangan, Mary Kay Moran,
Patricia Smalley, Gabrielle Smith, Linda Wolfe,
Johanna Zacharias
Copy Coordinator: Susan B. Galloway
Design Assistant: Anne B. Landry
Picture Coordinator: Elizabeth A. Dagenhardt

EDITORIAL OPERATIONS
Design: Ellen Robling (assistant director)
Copy Room: Diane Ullius
Editorial Operations: Caroline A. Boubin (manager)
Production: Celia Beattie
Quality Control: James J. Cox (director), Sally Collins
Library: Louise D. Forstall

Correspondents: Elisabeth Kraemer-Singh (Bonn); Margot Hapgood, Dorothy Bacon (London); Susan Jonas, Lucy T. Voulgaris (New York); Maria Vincenza Aloisi, Josephine du Brusle (Paris); Ann Natanson (Rome). Valuable assistance was also provided by: Cynthia Cochran, Margot Sider (Chicago); Ann Conner (San Francisco); Juliane Greenwalt (Detroit); Gayle Rosenberg (Los Angeles); Sue Wymelenberg (Boston).

Contents

America
1960-1970

SOAP OPERA ACTORS
FOR PEACE
Silent Vigil One Second
For Each Soldier Killed
In Vietnam

Peace vigil, New York, 1969.

Jogging for physical fitness, Des Moines, 1969.

Commencement at Wesleyan University, Connecticut, 1969.

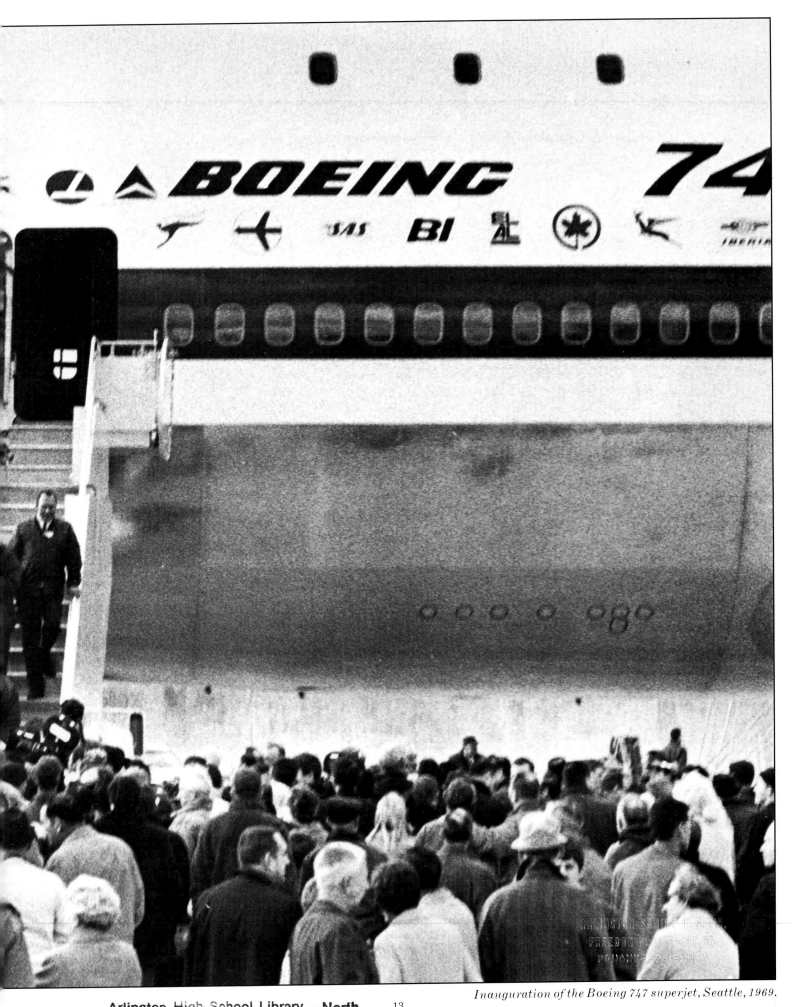

Inauguration of the Boeing 747 superjet, Seattle, 1969.

13

A cigar company's safe-smoking class, Philadelphia, 1963.

Civil rights march, Montgomery, Alabama, 1965.

Commuters on the Long Island Rail Road, 1966.

Surfing off Hermosa Beach, California, 1961.

High-rise patio living in Manhattan, 1963.

Give a damn.

The New Commitment

We stand today on the edge of a new frontier—the frontier of the 1960s, a frontier of unknown opportunities and perils, a frontier of unfulfilled hopes and threats.   JOHN F. KENNEDY, JULY 1960

It was an odd place to be, and an even stranger thing to be doing there. On a jungle river in Sarawak, on the north coast of Borneo, a 20-year-old American named Ed Price, wearing nothing but a wristwatch and a loincloth, paddled a native dugout canoe upstream into headhunter country. The canoe was laden with plant seed, fertilizer, bags of cement, fruit tree seedlings, baby chicks and rabbits. Price, a volunteer in the Peace Corps, was about to try a uniquely American experiment in improving the living standard of a village of Iban tribesmen. He was about to set up a 4-H club.

With his horn-rimmed glasses, crew cut and air of boyish earnestness, Price looked as though he belonged back home in Palatka, Florida, cramming for a physics exam or winging hook shots into a basket in the local gym. But like thousands of other Americans in the first years of the new decade, he felt a need, as he modestly explained, "to get out and do something constructive." This urge had carried him through a series of adventures more reminiscent of the rigorous life of the old frontier than of the split-level comforts of the world's richest nation. At a

Peace Corps training camp in Hawaii he had slept in a bamboo hut, lived off native roots and coconut milk, slogged through tidal swamps and up mountain ridges, learned to harvest rice in a paddy, and to speak the language and observe the customs of the Borneo jungles. Once in Sarawak, while showing the Ibans how to plant corn and build chicken coops—and in the process becoming the adopted son of a village chieftain—he caught two kinds of severe tropical disease.

Yet the hardships all seemed worthwhile. For Price had been caught up in a wave of energetic idealism that swept the nation during the early 1960s, washing away its previous mood of apathy and self-content. There was a feeling of commitment in the air. It welled up in a hundred different places, from college campuses to executive board rooms to the long corridors of government office buildings, and it embraced mail clerks and corporation presidents alike. It was reflected in the growing list of Peace Corps volunteers (more than 18,000 people applied in the organization's first year), in the scores of businessmen and university professors who flocked to Washington to join President John Kennedy's New

Frontier and in the soaring number of crusades, each with its slogans and posters, and buttons like the ones on these pages. The feeling of commitment would change, as the decade wore on, from optimism to doubt to disenchantment. But throughout, in ways that no one could have imagined a generation earlier, all kinds of people began to show—passionately and sometimes vocally—that they gave a damn.

Commitment in 1960 reached into the highest places in the land. Washington, D.C., on December 13, was bitter cold, with sharp, gusty winds and 20° temperatures. Despite the weather, the two figures standing on the front steps of the handsome brick house in Georgetown wore neither hats nor coats. Cold, brilliant sunlight glinted off the icicles hanging from the eaves above them, and on the street in front of the house a cluster of reporters and photographers rubbed their hands and stamped their feet in the snow. One of the men was 43-year-old John F. Kennedy, who had been elected President just five weeks earlier. The other was Robert S. McNamara, 44, who the day after Kennedy's election had himself been named president of the Ford Motor Company. In spite of the newness of this post, and the high salary that went with it, McNamara had agreed to quit, Kennedy told reporters, in order to become the country's next Secretary of Defense.

McNamara was a strange blend of organization man and intellectual. A Phi Beta Kappa from the University of California, he had risen to the top of the automobile industry through executive brilliance and hard, highly systematic work. With his slicked-down hair, rimless glasses and no-nonsense manner, he did not appear to be a man who was easily ruffled, or swayed by passion. But the week of his appointment as Defense Secretary had been one of dizzying surprises and intense soul-searching.

On the morning of December 7, McNamara received an unexpected phone call from John Kennedy's brother Robert, who wanted to set up an appointment in Detroit between the new Ford president and Sargent Shriver, a Kennedy in-law and aide. Shriver arrived from Washington that very afternoon. "I'm authorized to offer you a post in the cabinet," he said. "I'm authorized to accept 'Yes' as an answer, but I'm not authorized to accept 'No.'"

McNamara was stunned. "I'm not qualified," he protested. "I've an obligation to the Ford Motor Company. I've just been president four weeks."

The next morning McNamara flew to Washington to talk with John Kennedy in person. When the Ford executive cited his lack of government experience, Kennedy said, "I'm not aware of any school for cabinet officers." Then he paused and added with a wry smile, "or for Presidents either." McNamara left quietly by the back door to avoid reporters; he was charmed, impressed and for once in his life unsure of how to decide.

McNamara had powerful financial reasons for not leaving Ford: It would mean giving up almost five million dollars in salary, dividends and stock options over the next four years. But as he consulted with friends and read over Kennedy's campaign speeches, he began to feel a growing sense of excitement and adventure. At the Democratic Convention in July, Kennedy had described his New Frontier: "Not a set of promises, it is a set of challenges. It sums up not what I intend to offer the American people, but what I intend to ask of them." Already this challenge had attracted some of the best brains from the country's foremost universities. It was the kind of challenge that a man like McNamara, with his own keen intelligence and deep sense of duty, could not resist.

On February 1, 1960, in Greensboro, North Carolina, four determined young men sauntered into the local F. W. Woolworth store on South Elm Street, made a few small purchases and then sat down at the lunch counter for a cup of coffee. But the coffee never came.

The four youths, all freshmen at the nearby North Carolina Agricultural & Technical College, stayed there, without being served, until the store closed for the night. They knew beforehand that it would happen that way. For in North Carolina, where the patterns of racial segregation were deeply woven into the social fabric, Negroes simply did not sit down at lunch counters with white folks. And these four youths happened to be black.

Next morning they returned with five companions. They came back each day, with ever-growing reinforcements, until it seemed as though the entire college was trying to buy coffee at Woolworth's. The black students were quiet, orderly and remarkably cool, despite the malicious taunts of angry whites who stood by flipping cigarette butts at them and waving Confederate flags. Yet, as one of the youths said later, "That dime store down there was the birthplace of a whirlwind."

It was a whirlwind that tore across the nation. Within two weeks there were sit-ins in 15 cities in five Southern states. They spread from Woolworth to Kress, Liggett and Walgreen — anywhere that blacks were denied service. The movement swept north, and on March 23 divinity students at Yale University marched 300 strong through downtown New Haven to express their support. Three days later, 400 civil rights demonstrators from Harvard, Boston University, M.I.T. and Brandeis simultaneously picketed 12 Woolworth stores in Greater Boston.

Store managers tried a variety of gambits to stop the sit-ins. In some places they called the cops; a number of demonstrators were hauled off to jail on disorderly conduct charges. Elsewhere they raised their coffee prices to blacks to a dollar a cup. Some establishments simply closed down. One ingenious proprietor sidestepped the problem by unscrewing the seats at the lunch counter.

But still the protest gathered strength. It expanded during the spring and summer to read-ins in all-white libraries, sleep-ins in the lobbies of segregated motels, wade-ins at restricted beaches. And little by little, first in one community and then another, because of nameless and numberless people who gave a damn, the color bar began to edge downward.

Somewhere in the bamboo jungle of a tiny Asian country called South Vietnam, an American Army captain sat in a thatch-roofed hut, bent over a chessboard. In the intense humidity of the tropical night he wore shorts, sneakers and no shirt. At the first crackle of rifle fire, he said, "The Civil Guard's catching hell again." Then he grabbed his carbine and headed out into the darkness to help his encampment of South Vietnamese Army Rangers fend off an attack by Viet Cong guerrillas. For in the strange nonwar of the Vietnamese jungles, the captain was one of 200 soldiers of the U.S. Army's most elite corps, who in the fall of 1961 were quietly schooling local troops in the tricks of counterguerrilla warfare.

The U.S. Special Forces, to which the captain belonged, were generally considered to be the most highly disciplined, intensely professional soldiers that the United States had ever produced. Their particular patron was none other than President John Kennedy, who was attracted to anything expert, stylish and exceptional. Having read impressive books on guerrilla tactics by two Communists, China's Chairman Mao Tse-tung and Cuban military strategist Che Guevara, he had decided that the United States needed some guerrillas of its own; two months after his inauguration he asked Congress for $39 million, part of which was intended to revitalize America's languishing Special Forces program. He also overturned an order forbidding Special Forces soldiers to wear green berets as their official headgear. "They need something to make them distinctive," he said.

Distinctive they were, by dint of some of the most grueling training in the military. The Green Berets learned to jump from airplanes, blow up bridges, crack codes, remove an appendix and speak a variety of obscure languages. They mastered the arts of shooting a Chinese machine gun, of surviving unsupported in the jungle or desert, and of killing another man with their bare hands. At the Special Forces training camp at Fort Bragg, North Carolina, there was a six-foot-deep crater known as the Gladiator Pit. The trainees would leap in 60 at a time and battle each other—for kicks—until only one person remained in the pit. The result was a total soldier —tough, proficient, dedicated. "These men," said a Green Beret commander, Brigadier General William Yarborough, "are the Harvard Ph.D.'s of the Special Warfare art." And indeed, they seemed the perfect military reflection of the New Frontier.

They seemed also to be the perfect answer to Communist aggression in Southeast Asia. Secretly at first, and then openly, Kennedy sent Green Berets to South Vietnam and Laos to train indigenous troops. The men embarked with an almost missionary eagerness. For even though their business, ultimately, was killing, the Green Berets were idealists. The Latin inscription on their emblem read *De Oppresso Liber* —"To Liberate from Oppression." And each man was convinced that all the nasty tricks he had been taught would somehow help to set the world free.

On the afternoon of May 13, 1960, on the ornate steps of San Francisco's City Hall, a squad of frightened policemen battled 200 angry college students with fire hoses and nightsticks. The trouble had started when the House Committee on Un-American Activities, investigating Communism in California, subpoenaed a number of local schoolteachers and also a sophomore at the University of California who had all supposedly been active in leftist causes. Indignant at what seemed to be a violation of political freedom, busloads of students had driven over from the University of California at Berkeley to protest. No violence had been planned. But when the stu-

dents were denied entrance to the crowded hearing room, they tried to push their way in. A policeman was knocked down and beaten. Out came the hoses and billy clubs. The battle raged for half an hour, and when it was over, 12 people had been injured and 52 demonstrators were carted off to jail.

Nothing could have surprised the country more. Just a year earlier, President Clark Kerr of the University of California had predicted: "The employers will love this generation. . . . They are going to be easy to handle. There aren't going to be any riots." Now, however, the crusading spirit of the new decade had begun to galvanize the nation's campuses, and students were being caught up in spite of themselves. Said one youthful bystander at San Francisco, who had come to watch and had ended up by taking part: "I was a political virgin, but I was raped on the steps of City Hall." Social critic Jessica Mitford was less graphic but perhaps more pertinent

L.B.J. shows off his gall-bladder scar.

about the riot in an article in *The Nation:* "The current crop of students had gone far to shake the label of apathy and conformity that had stuck through the Fifties." The young generation, she continued, was committed to "shaping the future of the world."

And so it went in the first eager days of the 1960s. In schools and colleges, on jungle rivers, in military training camps, in the high reaches of government, the spirit of commitment burned.

Then came the Day of Drums.

The shock of the assassination of President Kennedy on November 22, 1963, in bright sunlight on a Dallas street, hit the nation with immediate and horrifying impact. Minutes after the spatter of rifle shots had slammed into the President as he rode in the back seat of an open convertible, the news was broadcast across the continent. During the next hour, while doctors at the Dallas hospital worked to revive the President's heart, millions of Americans hunched in agonized disbelief over their radio and TV sets. It was an hour that seemed months long.

When the doctors gave up, at approximately 1:20 in the afternoon, the nation reacted as though a great natural catastrophe, such as an earthquake or a flood, had struck. Bells began to toll, and stunned, silent throngs began gathering inside churches. A woman shopper in Lord & Taylor's department store in New York City fell to her knees in prayer. Hardly anyone spoke above a whisper. Those who did voiced a deep sense of disillusionment. Exclaimed John McCormack, the 71-year-old Speaker of the House of Representatives: "My God! My God! What are we coming to?" For the moment, no one seemed to know.

In the cabin of the Presidential jet plane at Love Field in Dallas, Vice President Lyndon Johnson took the oath of office as the country's next President. His hulking body sagged perceptibly, and his face was a grim white mask. A local federal judge, 67-year-old Sarah T. Hughes, administered the oath in a barely audible quaver. The 25 witnesses, mostly Kennedy aides, watched in pinched, somber silence. Some wept openly. Then, the ceremony over, the nation's 36th President issued his first executive order. "Let's get this goddam thing airborne," he said.

Back in the White House, Johnson moved decisively to assure the bewildered nation that the hopes and promises of the Kennedy years were not really dead. Five days after the assassination, he told Congress: "No words are strong enough to express our determination to continue the forward thrust of America that he began. . . . This is no time for delay. It is a time for action." And it seemed during the next few months that the new President, with his powerful ability to persuade, bargain and cajole, would accomplish feats of government beyond those of any predecessor since Franklin D. Roosevelt.

A renewed wave of optimism rolled across the nation as the 1964 Presidential elections approached. Not only would Johnson continue the New Frontier, but he would add a few humanitarian embellishments of his own under a fresh slogan, the Great Society. Already he had set in motion the most ambitious program of social improvement in 30 years, including a landmark education bill, a major civil rights bill and a series of anti-poverty projects. "The Great Society rests on abundance and liberty for all. It demands an end to poverty and racial injustice," he had told a graduating class at the University of Michigan in May 1964. "But that is just the beginning." The Great Society would also include an all-out attack on water pollution and urban decay.

Clearly the Great Society was what the nation wanted—at least in preference to the only alternative it was offered. Americans elected Johnson in November over conservative Republican candidate Barry Goldwater by 61 per cent of the vote—the largest plurality since the first Presidential voting statistics had been compiled in 1824.

The big, blustering Texan in the White House rode

high in the saddle through 1964 and into the summer of 1965. The President's fatherly demeanor, even though combined with a barnyard folksiness that once impelled him to show off the scar from a gall-bladder operation to newspaper photographers, gave the nation a fleeting sense of security. Many Americans agreed with White House aide Jack Valenti when he said, "I sleep each night a little better, a little more confidently because Lyndon Johnson is my president." This optimism persisted through May, even after Johnson, harkening to the ancient call of Manifest Destiny, shipped soldiers to the Dominican Republic to put down an attempted leftist coup d'état. It continued with only slight misgivings through July, when Johnson asked for a massive increase of U.S. troops in South Vietnam; the popularity polls that the President habitually carried around in his pocket showed that 70 per cent of the nation still liked him. Even in August, when angry blacks set fire to a Los Angeles ghetto called Watts, disillusionment had not yet reached the entire country.

But disillusionment came, strong and sudden. Despite the fine promises of the Great Society, the nation's cities were crumbling at an alarming rate. In July 1966, black ghettos burned in Cleveland and Chicago, and riots broke out in black communities across the nation. Civil rights workers in the South were beaten and shot at. Several were killed. At the same time, the casualty lists from Vietnam mounted painfully in a war that seemed to have no purpose and no end. To compound the problem, Johnson kept assuring the nation that nothing was really wrong. "The credibility gap is getting so bad, we can't even believe our own leaks," said Johnson's press secretary, Bill Moyers, just before he quit in December 1966. Violence continued through 1967, and the protests mounted as the Vietnam war dragged on. By the decade's end, the hopes and promises of its first bright years had turned to deep disenchantment, and giving a damn had become a bitter, angry thing.

Lapel buttons gave Americans of the 1960s a simple, direct way of expressing their views on all kinds of volatile issues.

Camelot

The White House on inauguration eve, 1961.

Period of Grace

Don't let it be forgot

That once there was a spot

For one brief shining moment

That was known as Camelot.

ALAN JAY LERNER

Once upon a time, for a thousand days, Jack and Jacqueline Kennedy lived in the White House and presided over their domain with a magical blend of elegance and vibrance. Never had a first family been so good-looking or seemed so young, so intelligent, so talented, so brimming with vitality. Nor had affairs of state, both social and political, been conducted with such style. Furthermore, the Presidential couple seemed confidently aware of the charismatic tone they were setting: a favorite Kennedy song—with the lines he loved best *(above)*—came from a current hit show identified with his regime, *Camelot*, the story of the mythical court of King Arthur.

The tone was set on the very first day, when Kennedy invited Robert Frost to his inaugural, and it carried through to a day very close to the end, when the young President told an audience at Amherst College that he looked forward to "an America which will not be afraid of grace and beauty."

As mistress of the White House, Jacqueline supervised an extensive restoration. "Everything in the White House must have a reason for being there," said the discriminating First Lady. For White House galas, she brought in string quartets, ballet companies and Shakespearean actors. Master cellist Pablo Casals gave a concert in the East Room and Igor Stravinsky was the guest of honor at a party to celebrate his 80th birthday. When 49 Nobel Prize winners came to dinner, the President turned a handsome phrase: "This is the most extraordinary collection of talent . . . that has ever been gathered together at the White House—with the possible exception of when Thomas Jefferson dined alone."

Even the workaday business of Washington was glamorized by a whole new breed of government servant—men as young and brainy and as full of vigor as the Kennedys themselves. They came from Harvard and M.I.T., from Detroit and Irish Boston, and they shared the President's belief that true happiness lay "in the full use of your powers along lines of excellence." They also shared his delight in physical activity. They sailed boats in gales, hurtled down ski slopes and played a solid game of tennis. After one particularly exhausting day of trailing the Camelot court at play, one reporter panted, "Touch football is what is done instead of sitting down."

To guests at one of five inaugural balls, the dashing new President exclaimed, "I don't know a better way to spend an evening."

"Let the word go forth from this time and place . . . that the torch has been passed to a new generation of Americans. . . . So let us begin anew. . . . Together let us explore the stars, conquer the deserts, eradicate disease, tap the ocean depths and encourage the arts and commerce. . . . All this will not be finished in the first one hundred days. . . . The energy, the faith, the devotion which we bring to this endeavor will light our country and all who serve it — and the glow from that fire can truly light the world.

JOHN F. KENNEDY, JANUARY 20, 1961

Kennedy delivers his inaugural address. "That speech he made out here," said Sam Rayburn, "was better than Lincoln."

The Kennedys await guests at a dinner for French dignitary André Malraux; later on, violinist Isaac Stern played. "Command

performances at the White House," noted a "New York Times" reporter, "have become almost as sought after as postmasterships."

❝*Eighty guests sat around small tables in the Blue Room, and there was dancing till three in the morning. Never had girls seemed so pretty, tunes so melodious, an evening so blithe and unconstrained.*

ARTHUR M. SCHLESINGER JR. OF A WHITE HOUSE
PARTY FOR PRINCE AND PRINCESS RADZIWILL

The poetry and music of Elizabethan England echoed in the White House tonight after a dinner for a monarch of a modern era.

THE NEW YORK TIMES ON A DINNER
FOR THE GRAND DUCHESS OF LUXEMBOURG

Jackie charms Frost, André Malraux, Leonard Bernstein.

Pablo Casals takes a bow in the East Room. "When I played at the White House," he said, "I was very happy in my heart."

❝ *The responsibilities . . . are greater than
I imagined them to be, and there
are greater limitations upon our ability
to bring about a favorable result. . . .
It is much easier to make the speeches than
it is to finally make the judgments,
because unfortunately your advisers are
frequently divided. If you take the
wrong course, and on occasion I have, the
President bears the burden of
the responsibility. . . . The advisers
may move on to new advice.*

JOHN F. KENNEDY, DECEMBER 16, 1962

The President's office, "the very center of all the action," also symbolized, said Ted Sorensen, "his own peace of mind."

J.F.K.'s closest confidant was Bobby, whom the President considered "the brother within."

> **"**The more people I can see, or the wider I can
> expose my mind to different ideas,
> the more effective I can be as President.*
>
> JOHN F. KENNEDY

J.F.K. is briefed by phone from the U.N.

"Whoever he's with, he's with them completely," said one admirer; here Kennedy confers with India's Prime Minister Nehru.

"The President loved the sea," wrote Taz Shepard, J.F.K.'s naval aide. *"The summers of his childhood were spent beside it, playing*

in the grass on the restlessly shifting dunes, wading among the rushes that grew in the warm waters of Nantucket Sound."

❝I do not think it altogether inappropriate to introduce myself. I am the man who accompanied Jacqueline Kennedy to Paris.

JOHN F. KENNEDY, JUNE 2, 1961

All free men, wherever they may live, are citizens of Berlin. And therefore, as a free man I take pride in the words, 'Ich bin ein Berliner.'

JOHN F. KENNEDY, JUNE 26, 1963

The evidence is in and the verdict is clear: 'Jah-kee' is a solid smash in Vienna.

RUSSELL BAKER, *THE NEW YORK TIMES*, JUNE 5, 1961

"I'd like to shake HER hand first," remarked Khrushchev.

The Kennedys dine at Elysée Palace. "Very, very welcome," said

48

At the theater (top) and a state dinner, a
stunning Jackie was the star attraction.

…e normally icy de Gaulle. "Charmante! Ravissante!" cried the French press.

49

To "The New York Times" the trip to Mexico seemed "more like a giant United States-Mexican fiesta than a state visit."

Visiting in Pakistan, Jackie rides with President Ayub.

❝*By the uncounted millions, Mexicans gave him and his pretty wife the warmest abrazo. Gnarled old peasant women thrust bunches of white flowers at the cavalcade as it passed; urchins broke from the throng squealing 'Meester Kennedy. Meester Kennedy.' One youngster even carried a reassuring sign: 'We play touch football.'*   TIME, JULY 6, 1962

Judging from their comments, many Indians who watched her thought they were seeing a Queen.
      THE NEW YORK TIMES, MARCH 18, 1962

With the folded flag from her husband's coffin beneath her arm, Jacqueline Kennedy grieves beside the President's grave.

A riderless horse and a reversed boot symbolize the murdered leader.

❝*Mary McGrory said to me that we'll never laugh
again. And I said, 'Heavens, Mary. We'll laugh again.
It's just that we'll never be young again.'*

DANIEL PATRICK MOYNIHAN, NOVEMBER 1963

Youth Trip

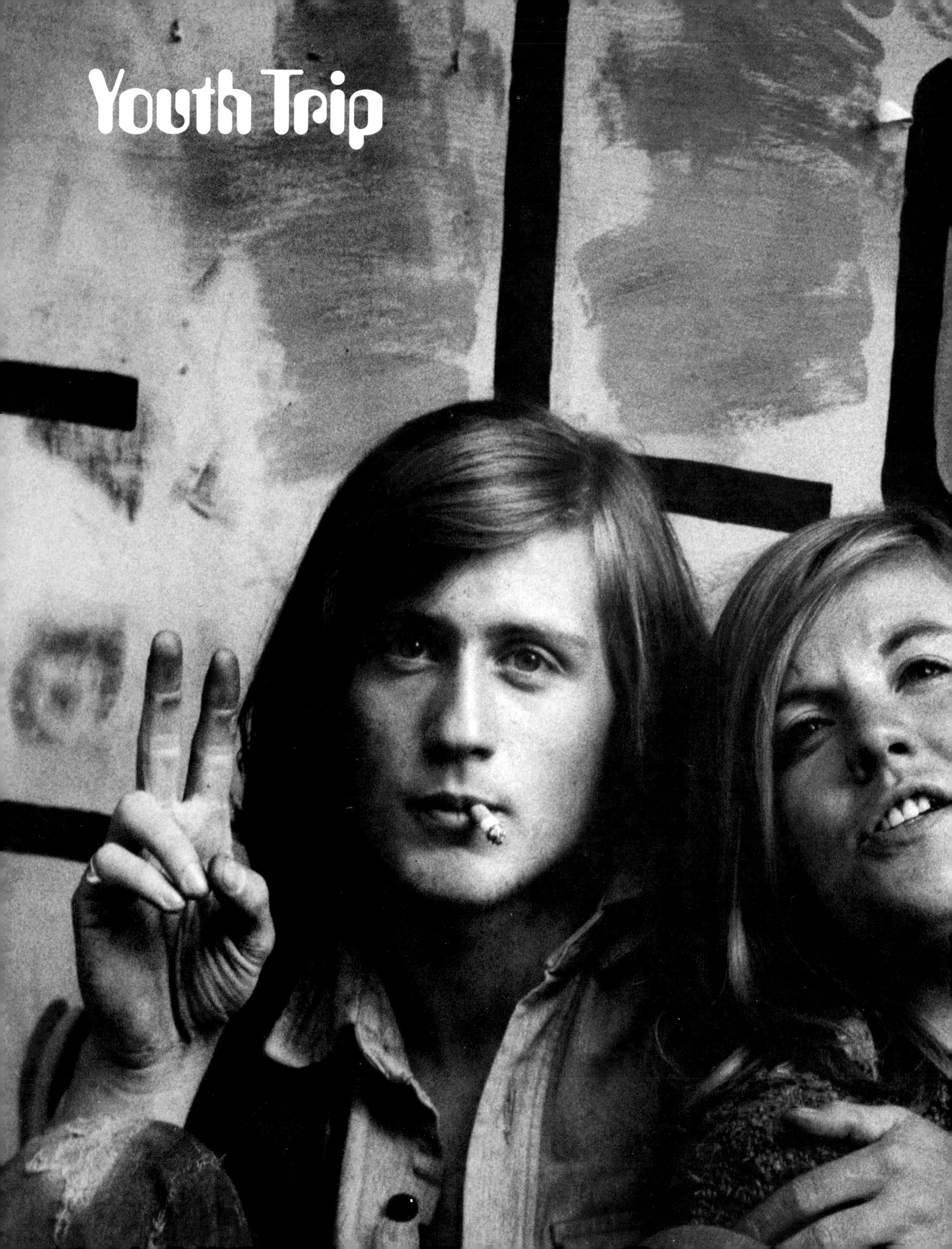

Manhattan love-in, 1968.

Love Children

What the world needs now/Is love sweet love
SONG BY BURT BACHARACH AND HAL DAVID, 1965

"Wow! Dig all the beautiful freaks!" It was summer of 1967, and the scene was the Haight-Ashbury section of San Francisco, epicenter of the hippie world, where people had come together by the thousands for a summer-long love-in. The man who spoke wore high buckskin boots with bells on them, shoulder-length hair and a flowing reddish beard that made him look like the Christ figure on a religious post card. A young ex-stockbroker, now a high priest of the love movement, he was grooving on the scene for the benefit of a friend, Professor Lewis Yablonsky of the sociology department at San Fernando Valley State College. Yablonsky had come with tape recorder and notebook to find out what the love movement was all about; he later put his findings into a book, *The Hippie Trip*. As Yablonsky watched that day, long-haired people wandered along Haight Street, clad in a brilliant motley of denim pants, flowered shirts, Mexican serapes, Navajo headbands and luminous body paint. The bluegrass aroma of marijuana smoke hung in the air, and the hard beat of acid-rock music blared from an open window in one of the frame houses that lined the street.

"Just let your light shine. That's about all you have to do," said the man with the belled boots.

Nearly all the people out on the street were in their late teens or early twenties. Some of them sat in groups on the pavement playing guitars. Others panhandled change from tourists, and one youth carried a sign that read, "Take a hippie to lunch."

To the trickle of smooth-shaven conventional citizens who came to gawk, it was a weird and rather unattractive scene, beyond explanation or reason. But to the colorful, shaggy mass of youngsters, the whole thing was perfectly summed up by the slogan on a poster pasted onto a wall: "Haight is love."

And love was indeed the dominant mood – not only physical love, though currents of eroticism hung like incense in the air, but a kind of indiscriminate, all-embracing brotherliness. People clustered together in circles to smoke marijuana joints and casually bedded down a dozen to a room in makeshift crash pads in neighborhood buildings. "I dig love," began an editorial in an underground newspaper. "I like to walk down the street where the vibrations are good. Those who go around hating are nowhere." A 20-

Caught up in loving spirit at New York City's Central Park, a boy paints a psychedelic design on his girl friend's sneaker.

year-old youth, interviewed by sociologist Yablonsky, offered this summation, amounting to a hippie credo: "God is. Love is. I am."

The same scene, and much the same sentiments, were repeated in other hippie capitals around the country. In New York City's East Village, bushy-haired teenagers wandered about the dingy streets and popped mescaline capsules in Tompkins Square Park. In Boston, they grouped together on the Common, where two centuries earlier colonial settlers had grazed cows; and they washed their clothes—often with themselves inside—in the Frog Pond. In the hills outside Los Angeles, in the Pennsylvania farmlands and in the New England woods, they lived together in tribal communes *(pages 70-75)*. A 20-year-old Californian offered this eulogistic description of such communal living. "All the girls are my wives and the guys are my brothers and the babies are mine and this is love—it is a true love."

The love movement, which reached its fullest blossoming in the hippie love-ins that were held during the summer of 1967, had been growing steadily since the middle of the decade. Its principal disciples, estimated at 300,000, called themselves Flower Children, Love Children, Gentle People and Free People. A fair number of the younger ones were bewildered high school kids who had run away from their parents. A few were hard drug users; others were decidedly psychotic. But according to a survey produced by Professor Yablonsky, more than half were reasonably mature people who had spent at least a year in college, and some had held responsible jobs in the business or academic world. Though they elected to live in poverty, the great majority came from fairly prosperous backgrounds; 70.8 per cent, according to the same survey, reported that their family's income was over $7,500. They were, in fact, renegades from the solid American middle class—a world that was socially respectable, economically secure, the breeding ground of the nation's future lawyers,

© Brothers Machine 1968

doctors and businessmen. Yet these young people had opted out in favor of a life they claimed was devoted to love of mankind, but which appeared, outwardly at least, to be more dedicated to squalor, irresponsibility and drugs.

WHY?

It was a question asked by parents, psychiatrists, sociologists, the news media, in fact the entire country. And it was a question that would have to be answered, for this vanguard of hippies was only the most tangible symbol of a new philosophy that cut to the very core of American life. For the first time in the nation's history, its basic Protestant ethic of hard work, respectability and competition for material success had been called massively to account. An entire generation—not only the love children, but the millions of young people who copied their clothing, hair styles, rock music and their general outlook —seemed to have found it wanting.

"What America? It's a shuck," said one young middle-class dropout. "It lacks something—like its original ideals and values," said another, a 22-year-old college graduate. Hip philosopher Stan Russell, one-time editor of the underground *The Los Angeles Oracle*, was more bitter: "The notion that the great plastic society is the only reality, and anything other than that is a drop-out culture is one of the crazy, insane, lunatic notions indulged in by its leaders."

In their questioning of the plastic society, some of the Gentle People gave up on peaceful love as a social cure, and they were caught up in the more violent political protests of the New Left. In a demonstration against Establishment politics at the 1968 Chicago Democratic Convention, some 700 members of the new generation and 200 police were injured; and in May 1969, during a controversy in Berkeley over a vacant lot occupied by local youths and college students who intended to make from it a "people's park," one man was killed and 60 were hurt.

But the true Flower Children never abandoned their basic credo of nonviolence, and while their brothers and sisters battled the police, the others sat back and waited, sure that in the end love would triumph. "All political systems are on the way out," said singer Arlo Guthrie, a hippie folk hero of American youth. "We're finally gonna get to the point where there's no more bigotry or greed or war. Peace is on the way. . . . People are simply gonna learn that they can get more by being groovy than being greedy."

There is something about the temper and quality of these people, a gentleness, a quietness, an interest — something good.   EPISCOPAL BISHOP JAMES PIKE

They took their tactics from Gandhi, their idealism from philosophy class and their money from Daddy.   MICHIGAN DAILY

[They are] a red warning light for the American way.   HISTORIAN ARNOLD TOYNBEE

God knows many of them are fools, and most of them will be sellouts but they're a better generation than we were.   PLAYWRIGHT LILLIAN HELLMAN

I have no objection to any herd of semi-domesticated animals roaming the country, uttering their mating cries and scratching their pelts, as long as they avoid centers of civilization and congregate only in college auditoriums.   CARTOONIST AL CAPP

It is not that what is done among the young is different or extreme; it is simply that what is done feels differently in quality, in resonance. It is a sense of warmth, of slowness and delight that seems to enter the flesh and abide there.   AUTHOR PETER MARIN

Kids today are detestable, and thank God mine are grown up. You couldn't give me another one. And it's no good saying that the ones you read about are a minority. They're not a minority if they're all yours and you have to wait for the car to get home to know your daughter hasn't got pregnancy or leprosy.   COMEDIAN GROUCHO MARX

We all live in a yellow submarine,

Yellow submarine, yellow submarine

As we live a life of ease

Ev'ry one of us has all we need

Sky of blue and sea of green

In our yellow submarine

"YELLOW SUBMARINE"
BY JOHN LENNON AND PAUL McCARTNEY

The Happiest People

No one proclaimed the message of love and happy living to American youth more beguilingly than four mop-haired rock singers from Liverpool, England, who called themselves The Beatles. Musical successors of 1950s American rock and roll, they added a note of irreverent, childlike whimsy that seemed to captivate every youngster in the world. After the release of their first big hit, "She Loves You," in 1963, Beatlemania spread like measles. Young people copied their mod clothing *(page 107)* and sheepdog haircuts, and scores of American rock groups developed a homespun version of the Liverpool sound.

Hefty doses of the hippie doctrine of love, freedom and innocence cropped up in many Beatles' lyrics. "All You Need is Love" is the title of one hit. Another, "Strawberry Fields Forever," evokes the same kind of never-never dreamland produced by a trip on drugs. But even when referring to explosive subjects like drugs, the four Liverpudlians maintained their endemically light, joyful touch, as described below in excerpts from a review of a Beatles movie, a rollicking cartoon fantasy entitled *Yellow Submarine.*

Like "Alice in Wonderland," the "Yellow Submarine" possesses all the impudent charm and pazzaz that appeal to the universal human thirst for simple lunacy. Visually, it is a dazzling, animated stream of leaping colors, exploding designs and zappy characters. . . .

Beyond the drawings, tunefulness, Beatle wit and "Submarine's" totally preposterous freshness, there is the power of the Beatles themselves. With their infectious influence on public thought, this film may be the first in a whole new eruption of spontaneous glee.

WILLIAM HEDGEPETH IN *LOOK* MAGAZINE

Beatles John Lennon, Paul McCartney, George Harrison and Ringo Starr cavort in a scene from "Yellow Submarine."

Got no deeds to do
No promises to keep
I'm dappled and drowsy and ready to sleep
Let the morning time drop all its petals on me
Life, I love you
All is groovy

"THE 59TH STREET BRIDGE SONG (FEELIN' GROOVY)"
BY PAUL SIMON

A pre-hippie attends a jazz festival in California

Feathers, finery, bubbles and beads are worn at a Los Angeles love-in.

Crowned with flowers, folk singer Arlo Guthrie and his bride Jackie are serenaded by Judy Collins at their outdoor wedding.

Why don't we sing this song all together?
Open our heads, let the pictures come
And if we close all our eyes together
Then we will see where we all come from

The Super Love-In

In the summer of 1969, on a rented 600-acre dairy farm near the town of Woodstock, New York, an open-air community of 400,000 young people materialized for three dizzying days to listen to rock and blues music, to wear funny clothes or no clothes at all, to talk, sing, dance, clap hands, to drink beer and smoke pot and make love—but mostly to marvel again and again at the fact that they were all there together. "Far out—even Billy Graham doesn't draw *that* many people!" exclaimed one youngster, taking in the vast sea of humanity, almost all of it between the ages of 15 and 25.

Despite traffic jams, lack of food, shelter and sanitation, and blustering rainstorms that turned the crowded hillsides to mud, there was not a single fist fight nor even a disparaging word. In fact, all was love. Members of the Hog Farm and other communes *(pages 70-75)* set up free kitchens, gave first aid and helped kids down from bad drug trips. When it finally ended after 60 wet, wonderful hours, Woodstock had gone into the national vocabulary as the biggest, loudest, lovingest youth happening of the decade.

What made it wonderful was the fact that all those people could get along together without one black eye, one cut lip. That's what went down—the kids respected the cops for doing their thing (and doing it well, too) and the cops respected the kids for not running wild even though the conditions were terrible. You know, they could have started burnin' stuff down, but they just sat there and were grooving with each other.

FOLK SINGER ARLO GUTHRIE

Wow! Phhhew! I mean like wow! Phhhew!

SINGER RICHIE HAVENS, LOOKING AT THE CROWD

At Woodstock, the youngsters sit, sprawl, rap, skinny-dip, huddle in the rain, slide in the mud and sleep wherever they can.

Woodstock's landscape of bodies stretched for 35 acres from a stage, where rock music blasted out of speakers atop towers.

Alone and far from home, hippie kids think it over on the sidewalks and park benches of New York City's East Village.

People try to put us down

Just because we get around

Things they do look awful cold

Hope I die before I get old

"MY GENERATION" BY PETER TOWNSHEND

How does it feel, how does it feel

To be without a home

Like a complete unknown

LIKE A ROLLING STONE?

"LIKE A ROLLING STONE" BY BOB DYLAN

Bob Dylan, rock-poet of the Now generation, in New York.

Some members of the Hog Farm commune congregate in the kitchen of a borrowed loft apartment during a New York visit.

The New Utopias

Not since Brook Farm and other utopian communities of the 19th Century had there been such a revival of experiments, especially among the young, in dropping out of straight society to find more meaningful ways of living with nature and one another. Scores of small communities sprang up all over the country, from Drop City, U.S.A., a colony of 20 artists and writers in geodesic domes on the Colorado desert, to The Church People, a band of 20 refugees living in a deconsecrated church in Massachusetts. One of the most colorful of the new communes was the Hog Farm, a peripatetic group of about 30 to 50 people who originally got together under an ex-coffeehouse comedian named Hugh Romney to build a ragtag gathering of tents and shacks in the foothills near Los Angeles. Soon the group, which included actors, musicians and film technicians, bought some old buses, painted them in psychedelic colors, rigged the interiors with bunks and started traveling to rock festivals all the way from Woodstock, New York, to Orlando, Florida. When the spirit moved them, the Hog Farmers temporarily abandoned the buses to crash at friends' houses or apartments in San Francisco or New York *(left and overleaf)*. In the excerpt that follows, from an underground paper called *The Realist*, Romney extols the Farmers' life.

The Hog Farm is an expanded family, a mobile hallucination, a sociological experiment, an army of clowns. We are 50 people on a perpetual trip, citizens of earth. We have six converted school buses, some vans and pickups, one for our pet pig Pigasus, who now weighs 400 pounds and has learned to roll over. It

Text continued on page 74.

Hog Consciousness—a true feeling of loving and sharing—is high around the dinner table, with the kids joining right in.

Exhausted by a day of full living, members crash happily together on an assortment of beds, mattresses and blankets.

seems like it was almost yesterday. We had been liv-ing on this pig farm about two years. Just a few people in the beginning, in the mud hanging windows on the wind, fixin' up the joint after years of vandalism and neglect. Also our bodies and brains, trying to get it to-gether, some kind of Hog Consciousness. And others started comin' in. All kinds of people....

To equalize the division of work, we instituted the dance master program. Our dance master ran the farm and the dance mistress ran the kitchen, and each day it was some different person working off this wheel with everybody's name. We could feed 30 people on $3 a day combined with a garbage run at local supermar-kets. In California they throw away a lot of stuff, tons of near fresh fruits and vegetables plus scooter pies and other goodies.

Each Sunday [has] a theme. Always a celebration. Lots of food and music. One Sunday it's kites. Anoth-er is Mud Sunday. And Dress Like Kids Day with silly shorts and water pistols and a formal croquet party held in a pig pen, the hog farm state fair with the bake-off and freak show and who can stay under water the longest. [One Sunday] I have my first official wedding to perform.... Marrying Paul Foster to anything could prove to be a scene. The ceremony must be ac-tive, fast and groovy. Paul will wear ice skates for the occasion....

[One] night a baby is born in camp, in the back of a 1952 International Harvester truck. Her name is Cueva and she weighed about 6 pounds. Ken Babbs played the doctor. Somebody else played the guitar.

After a meal, members of the Hog Farm family practice togetherness by doing a little impromptu singing with their dog.

Have you ever been to electric ladyland?

The magic carpet waits for you,

so don't be late

I want to show you different emotions

I want to ride you

through the sounds and motions

"HAVE YOU EVER BEEN (TO ELECTRIC LADYLAND)"
BY JIMI HENDRIX

Psychedelia

One dazzling haven sought by the way-out young rebels of the '60s was immersion in some sort of psychedelic experience. According to *The Random House Dictionary*, psychedelic meant "intensely pleasureful perception of the senses." In the jargon of the rebels themselves, psychedelic was "something beautiful man, like it blows your mind." This mind-blowing adventure could be triggered by music, sexuality, drugs, fool-the-eye art, or even by extended meditation into the esoteric reaches of astrology or Hindu mysticism. It could also be triggered by a wild jumble of multi-media distortions hurled at the senses of patrons at psychedelic rock palaces. In San Francisco, the far-out place to be was Fillmore West; New York had half a dozen spots, including the Electric Circus (whose light show is explained below by its operators), Fillmore East and the Group Image. With variations, all these emporiums presented dazzling, nonstop light shows that melted across walls and ceilings. Keyed to the lights were usually the pounding, twanging songs of various rock groups. One young enthusiast described the effect thus: "It's like wherever you stand, you're somewhere else."

This is an environment. It's like the advent of Feelys in "Brave New World." Maybe we could show Nassau and program the sea smell and soft breezes. With five senses you learn more than with two senses. With five senses, it's happening. Our motto comes from the novelist Hermann Hesse: "We are in a magic theater, a world of pictures not reality/Tonight at the magic theater for madmen only/the price of admission your mind." THE PABLO LIGHT SHOW

Ever-shifting lights and rock music combine to create a hallucinatory world for patrons of the Group Image in Manhattan.

RAYMUNDO DE LARRAIN

Mirrors multiply the image of singer Jimi Hendrix, providing a visual parallel for the psychedelic sound of his rock music.

Picture yourself in a boat on a river

With tangerine trees and marmalade skies

Somebody calls you, you answer quite slowly

A girl with kaleidoscope eyes

Cellophane flowers of yellow and green . . .

"LUCY IN THE SKY WITH DIAMONDS"
BY JOHN LENNON AND PAUL McCARTNEY
Copyright © 1967 Northern Songs Limited.
Used by permission. All rights reserved.

A California hippie adorns his car with a gaudy blend of organic designs and astrological and Oriental religious symbols.

Garish psychedelic posters, some of them frankly suggestive, advertise light-and-music shows in San Francisco.

*Performances like the one at right set off a great
controversy over on-stage nudity,
whose meaning to young rebels was explained
(below) by a leading practitioner.*

I came to the theater, as others have, by way of painting and dance. As a painter, I had for my heroes
Botticelli and Modigliani; as a dancer, Isadora Duncan, and so the carry-over on to the stage of the nude
body seemed to me not only stylistically expressive,
but a perfect extension of my beliefs.

I considered (and still do) the naked human body
the height of beauty, innocence and truth. Vietnam,
Chicago and Berkeley made me realize that my body
could not be my own "property" any longer, and that
trust and vulnerability were our only salvation. I
wished to say that, in reaching the natural end of their
emancipation, women of my generation could no longer consider themselves as "property."

Now, as with so many other experiments, nudity
has become a commercial product. The young people,
however, have picked up on the notion that physical
nudity was only the opening artistic gesture, which,
for them, helped to form an attitude of spiritual na-
kedness in opposition to our national endeavors. . . .

When we come to the day when no one in this country feels funny about taking off his clothes, then we've
come to a healthy time. I'm embarrassed by nudity
—but that's what it's all about. I want to be embarrassed. I want you to be vulnerable to my embar-
rassment and then maybe we can talk as soul mates.

ACTRESS SALLY KIRKLAND, *THE NEW YORK TIMES*, 1969

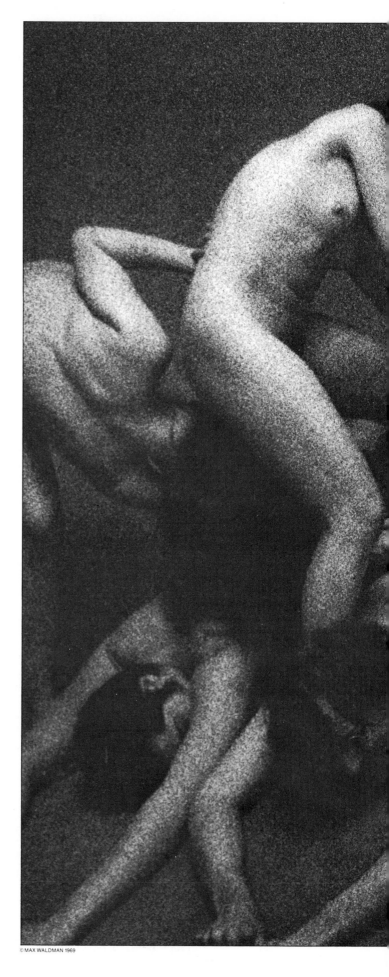

© MAX WALDMAN 1969

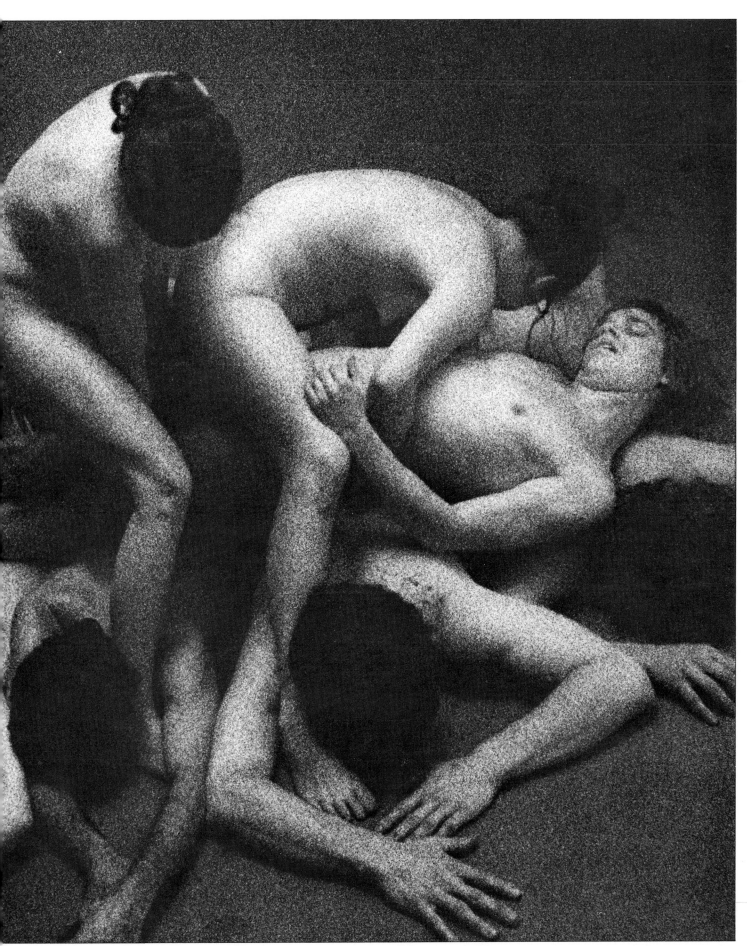

In an off-Broadway production of "Dionysus in '69," a group of nude actors move through an exaltation of the act of birth.

Eight miles high,
And when you touch down
You'll find that
It's stranger than known.

The Drug Cult

In its sustained and often frantic search for a new freedom, American youth in the '60s turned to drugs in staggering quantities. Dr. Henry Brill, chairman of the American Medical Association's committee on drug dependence, estimated that from 1960 to 1970 the number of Americans who had sampled marijuana had increased from a few hundred thousand to 8,000,000. The majority of the new users ranged from 12-year-old school kids to college seniors.

To their elders, these youngsters seemed, like lemmings, to have embarked on a vast and incomprehensible march toward their own destruction. But to the kids themselves—though most steered clear of the hard, addictive narcotics like heroin—the use of marijuana, hashish and even the perhaps psychologically and genetically dangerous LSD was indeed an expression of their new religion of love and freedom, of which drugs were the sacrament. In fact, the drug cult had its hymns to hallucinatory joy sung by rock groups; and it even boasted a self-appointed high priest named Dr. Timothy Leary, a dropout from Harvard University, where he had lectured in psychology. Leary spent most of the decade trying—and with some success—to convince his flock of the spiritual uplift to be had from the use of drugs *(below).*

LSD is Western yoga. The aim of all Eastern religion, like the aim of LSD, is basically to get high; that is, to expand your consciousness and find ecstasy and revelation within.   DR. TIMOTHY LEARY

This is one of the profound insights you can have on LSD, you experience yourself as God.
LEWIS YABLONSKY, *THE HIPPIE TRIP*

A rock group, The Doors, poses as if in a mind-expanding trance

Drug advocate Timothy Leary meditates below bumper stickers touting marijuana.

Devotees of the god Krishna sing a chant in New York. Their pigtails enable him to pull them "into greater consciousness."

Hare Krishna, Hare Krishna
Krishna Krishna, Hare Hare
Hare Rama, Hare Rama
Rama Rama, Hare Hare

HINDU INVOCATION

Hindu wise man, the guru Maharishi, meets the U.S. press.

The chant above repeats different names for the
godhead of an Oriental religion embraced
by American youth in the '60s. Another popular
mystical movement was led by the bearded
sage Maharishi Maresh Yogi (above), who wowed his
American audience on a visit in 1968.

The nature of outer life is activity. Inner life is all si-
lent and quiet. At this quiet end is absolute being, non-
changing, transcendental bliss.

MAHARISHI MARESH YOGI

So far, man, it's just all peace and energy. Since we
met the guru, we've got to the subtler states of being,
man. He's fantastic.

BRIAN AND CARL WILSON, SINGERS WITH THE BEACH BOYS

Once the soul of India gets into you, it sits on your
shoulder all the time. ACTRESS SHIRLEY MAC LAINE

When the moon is in the seventh house
And Jupiter aligns with Mars
Then peace will guide the planets
And love will steer the stars.
This is the dawning of the Age of Aquarius,
The Age of Aquarius.
Harmony and understanding
Sympathy and trust abounding
No more falsehoods or derisions
Golden living dreams of visions
Mystic crystal revelation
And the mind's true liberation.

"AQUARIUS" BY JAMES RADO,
JEROME RAGNI AND GALT MACDERMOT

The Broadway hit "Hair" unleashed a young cast who acted a wild musical sum-up of their generation's ideals and protests.

The murder of Lee Harvey Oswald, 1963.

Assassins

Terror and Doubt

All I can say is, good Lord, what is this all about? We could continue our
prayers that it would never happen again, but we did that before.

RICHARD CARDINAL CUSHING, ARCHBISHOP OF BOSTON, JUNE 5, 1968

On the afternoon of November 22, 1963, a few hours after President John F. Kennedy had been assassinated in Dallas, a postman in Greenwich, Connecticut, was making his rounds. At the stops along his route, he told a reporter later that day, "the housewives talked about it just as if they lost their son." The overwhelming emotion throughout the land on that bleak Friday was one of deep personal sorrow. But the personal feelings were mixed with national soul-searching and a sense that there was something deeply wrong within the country. "America wept tonight," wrote *New York Times* correspondent James Reston, "not alone for its dead young President, but for itself. The grief was general, for somehow the worst in the nation had prevailed over the best."

And more was yet to come. Two days later the man arrested for shooting the President, 24-year-old Lee Harvey Oswald, was himself killed when a Dallas nightclub owner, Jack Ruby, shot the suspect point-blank in full view of millions of stunned Americans who were watching live TV coverage of the assassination's aftermath.

Still it was not over. In April 1968 civil rights leader Martin Luther King Jr. was killed in Memphis, Tennessee, by a 40-year-old ex-convict, James Earl Ray. Then in June Senator Robert F. Kennedy fell under the bullets of a third assassin, Sirhan Bishara Sirhan, a 24-year-old Jordanian immigrant.

"What in the name of God has happened to us?" asked Senator Mike Mansfield. In public life and private, everyone had an answer. "President Kennedy," said New Orleans District Attorney Jim Garrison, "was killed for one reason: because he was working for a reconciliation with the U.S.S.R. and Castro's Cuba." "Ray was a dupe," said former Mayor Arthur Hanes of Birmingham, and the killing had to do with "international politics." Sirhan, said Los Angeles Mayor Sam Yorty, "was inflamed by contacts with the Communist party." "It's a conspiracy of the white power structure," said Floyd McKissick, former head of the Congress of Racial Equality.

Such observations—and the dark suspicion of a sinister rightist or leftist conspiracy of assassination—haunted Americans from the moment of John F. Kennedy's death. And almost to the end of the decade, the country went on probing for an explanation.

Text continued on page 97.

Ethel Kennedy fends off crowds around the body of her husband, the third national leader assassinated in the decade.

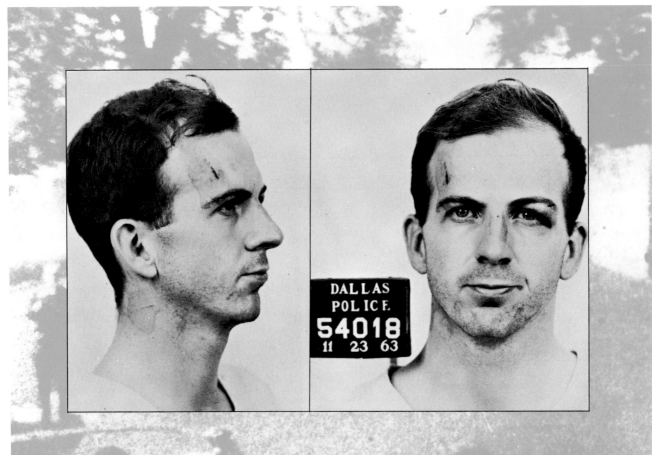

DALLAS
POLICE
54018
11 23 63

Name: *LEE HARVEY OSWALD*

Date of birth: *October 18, 1939*

Place of birth: *New Orleans, La.*

Physical characteristics: *Height, 5′.9″; Weight, 160 lbs.; Hair, brown and slightly kinky; Eyes, blue-gray; Build, slight.*

Idiosyncrasies: *Lean face; dark, ample eyebrows; prominent forehead; tight, crimped mouth; small, weak chin. Arrogant gestures alternating with calm self-possession.*

Family background: *Father, an insurance salesman, died two months before Oswald's birth. Mother worked; was "so wrapped up in her own problems she never really saw her son's," according to a probation officer.*

Personality traits: *Shy and awkward; unmannerly, opinionated, contrary, resentful, suspicious, withdrawn. Left school after ninth grade, and at age 17 enlisted in Marines; there he was unpopular and earned* the nickname *"Ozzie Rabbit."* At 19 sought and got transfer to the inactive reserve, saying he had to care for his mother. Promptly emigrated to U.S.S.R. Arriving in Moscow, applied for Russian citizenship, but failed to get it; later wrote that he was being held in the U.S.S.R. against his *"will and expressed desires."* Returned home after two and a half years, bringing a Russian wife and four-month-old daughter—but still could find no niche. Was hired and fired from series of jobs; tried and failed to go to Cuba. Built up a jumbled array of grudges; thought of people as *"pawns locked in a system"*; saw himself faced with an *"enemy"* with whom he intended to grapple.

Brushes with the law: *Appeared before Children's Court at 13; twice court-martialed in Marine Corps, first for possessing a pistol, later for challenging his sergeant to a fight.*

Name: *JAMES EARL RAY*
Date of birth: *March 10, 1928*
Place of birth: *Alton, Ill.*
Physical characteristics: *Height, 5' 11"; Weight, 165 lbs.; Hair, brown and straight; Eyes, blue; Build, slight.*
Idiosyncrasies: *Long, thin nose; protruding left ear; loping, uncoordinated walk. Difficulty looking anyone square in the eye; flinched when lying, as if expecting a clout.*
Family background: *Father was shiftless and generally unemployed, with a record of arrests for larceny and forgery, and a predilection for assuming aliases (Rayns, Raynes, Ryan), which mother and children also adopted. Mother was an alcoholic, a recluse and sometime streetwalker. Family, which eventually numbered nine children, lived in poverty, crowded into one room, without enough to eat; sometimes ripped out floors for firewood, sometimes huddled in bed all day to keep warm. Ray, in first grade, stole school-lunch money from teacher's desk; his younger brothers John Larry and Gerry were sent to reformatories at 19 and 14 respectively, both for robbery.*
Personality traits: *Shy; smouldered quietly when prodded, then exploded and fought to win. Bent on rising above environment; in the Army and on jobs as a stock boy and gas station attendant, he saved his pay, dreaming of buying own business, yet seemed to want to be thought a dangerous felon. Hated blacks. In prison, turned hypochondriac, took to speaking of his "solar plexus," "tachycardia," "intracranial tension."*
Brushes with the law: *Several prison terms for burglaries. Escaped from Missouri Penitentiary in April 1967; remained at large until captured after King assassination.*

Name: *SIRHAN BISHARA SIRHAN*
Date of birth: *March 19, 1944*
Place of birth: *Jerusalem*
Physical characteristics: *Height, 5' 3"; Weight, 120 lbs.; Hair, dark and curly; Eyes, dark; Build, slight and wiry.*
Idiosyncrasies: *Thin and nervous, sometimes inclined to sudden bursts of temper, other times oddly quiet for long periods.*
Family background: *Parents were Jordanian Christians; lived in poverty in two rooms, supported for the most part by Lutheran Church charity. Mother was dominant figure in family and Sirhan went with her everywhere; father was violent, with a sadistic streak—beat the children frequently and once burned Sirhan's heels with a hot iron. In 1957, when Sirhan was almost 13, family emigrated to U.S., settled—without becoming assimilated—in Los Angeles, in ethnically mixed, lower-middle-class neighborhood. After seven months the father abandoned the family, returned to Jordan and subsequently divorced the mother.*
Personality traits: *Few if any friends, but kept a diary in which he entered names of boys and girls whom he evidently wished to have as friends. Hated Zionists and Jews, whose treatment of Arabs he equated with Nazi treatment of Jews. Proud of not being a U.S. citizen, boasted of being Jordanian Arab. Angry and resentful of the rich, the successful and those in authority. In Pasadena City College, which he attended for a year and a half, said he wanted to be a journalist, diplomat, or teacher; later gave up those ideas to try to be a jockey, at which he failed. Talked of going back to Jordan and being somebody big, helping his people.*
Brushes with the law: *None*

Searches into the lives of the assassins proved nothing except that the triggermen were all losers. Yet from even this fragile common denominator some conclusions were drawn. "We're not a melting pot," said Dr. David Abrahamsen of Brandeis University; "we're a damned pressure cooker. Our society is built on success. If you don't have it, you're frustrated."

A government official voiced another theory, that assassination was spreading by contagion—and indeed there were figures to support that view. The Secret Service disclosed in January 1968 that the number of persons arrested annually for threatening the President's life had jumped by more than 500 per cent since November 1963.

The most massive probe into the subject of assassination was that done by the Warren Commission, the official body named by President Lyndon Baines Johnson to investigate the murder of John Kennedy. The Commission, under Chief Justice Earl Warren, spent 10 months hearing 552 witnesses give 10 million words of testimony that yeilded 26 volumes (18,000 pages) of records. Out of that opus came the shorter (888-page) Warren Report, which concluded that President Kennedy had been shot by Oswald acting by himself.

When the Warren Report was first published in September 1964, most Americans seemed willing to accept its conclusions. But some were so frustrated with the official explanations ("For people who really have an intellect it must be the most exquisite agony to read the pile of crap that they call the Warren Report," said an Oklahoma housewife) that they took to pondering the President's assassination on their own and seeking their own solutions. Some of the doubters were professional men with an ax to grind and an eye for profits. Others were amateur sleuths with a fondness for working at puzzles.

The amateurs built up extensive libraries that included newspaper clippings, maps of Dallas and the fast-proliferating books on the subject of the assassination. Most of the buffs even owned copies—at $76 a set—of the 26 volumes amassed by the Warren Commission. Their great fascination with the subject amounted to an obsession. "There's a fantastic way," said Josiah Thompson, a young Haverford College existential philosophy professor, "in which the assassination becomes a religious event. There are relics, and scriptures, and even a holy scene—the killing ground. People make pilgrimages to it."

Some of those investigating the assassination made money on the hobby. Mark Lane, a New York lawyer who had unsuccessfully offered himself to the Warren Commission as defense counsel for Oswald, published *Rush to Judgment*, which accused the Commission of having predetermined the verdict and quickly hit the bestseller lists. So did another inquiry, written by Edward Jay Epstein, a youthful Cornell University scholar who turned a master's thesis into a readable trade book, *Inquest*. And there were dozens of others, each of them touting a special message; by May 1967 there were, according to *Esquire* magazine, no fewer than 60 different versions of the President's assassination being peddled.

Dollars were not the only bait; there was also political capital to be made. The star performer on the political scene was District Attorney Jim Garrison of New Orleans, a six-foot six-inch 240-pounder known as the Jolly Green Giant. "My staff and I solved the assassination weeks ago," Garrison said in early 1967 and overnight found himself a national figure. He arrested an urbane New Orleans businessman, Clay Shaw, accusing him of having conspired with a clique of anti-Castro Cubans and disenchanted ex-CIA men to kill the President. Shaw, who had built the New Orleans International Trade Mart, had been voted New Orleans' most distinguished citizen of 1965. Holding out this juicy bait, Garrison won an eager audience that quickly spread beyond New Orleans. A Harris poll in May 1967 indicated that across the nation doubters of the Warren Report had risen from

44 to 66 per cent, and many of those thought that Garrison "had something."

Shaw's trial was postponed again and again on technicalities; while it was stalled, the assassinations of Martin Luther King and Robert Kennedy frightened more people into crediting the Garrison charges of conspiracy. But when the case finally came to court in January 1969, after nearly two years of accusations by Garrison, it fizzled as suddenly as it had begun—and Garrison lost his political gamble. The witnesses he had mustered proved so ineffectual that the jury acquitted Shaw after less than an hour's deliberation. By that time, the defendant was $100,000 poorer, thanks to the cost of his trial. But he accepted his misfortune with philosophic aplomb. Asked if he had any thoughts on the Garrison episode, he replied: "When death comes to a great leader, a prince, you expect it to come with black balloons, and the full panoply. It's hard to accept that this handsome young man, this great leader of the world, was struck down by a sorry little loser crouched behind a stack of cardboard boxes."

Yet eventually the nation did come to accept that fact—not only as it pertained to Oswald, but with reference to the others as well. William Bradford Huie, a free-lance writer who contracted for the book and movie rights to James Earl Ray's life and spent a year pursuing the theory that Ray was in cahoots with a mysterious conspirator named "Raoul," eventually declared: "I have been unable to come up with one shred of evidence that anyone else but Ray is involved in the murder of Dr. King." Sirhan, too, was written off as a mixed-up loner.

At decade's end conspiracy theories had subsided. But few who lived through the 1960s would forget the fears aroused by the assassin's form of violence; and none would ever be altogether rid of the deep awareness that something was wrong in the nation. Some of the thoughts expressed at home and overseas at the times of the killings are recorded below.

In no nation on earth is shooting people made so glamorously attractive by the media and nowhere else is it so easy for every nut to get a gun for that form of participatory democracy.

ABC COMMENTATOR HOWARD K. SMITH

To the rest of the world the United States must look like a giant insane asylum where the inmates have taken over. COLUMNIST ART BUCHWALD

The obvious question is—were there Communists involved? SENATOR JAMES O. EASTLAND

Only the triggerman in this monstrous crime has been convicted. In more than a rhetorical sense, the nation, which permitted rampant opposition to the aspirations of Dr. King and his people, is the real culprit. NAACP EXECUTIVE SECRETARY ROY WILKINS

What is wrong with America is that white America doesn't want to admit it is wrong.

NAACP FIELD DIRECTOR CHARLES EVERS

Two hundred million Americans didn't do this. One young man did it. GOVERNOR RONALD REAGAN

In the "freest" nation in the world murder has become a political tool. EAST GERMAN NEWS AGENCY

Let us, for God's sake, resolve to live under the law.
PRESIDENT LYNDON BAINES JOHNSON

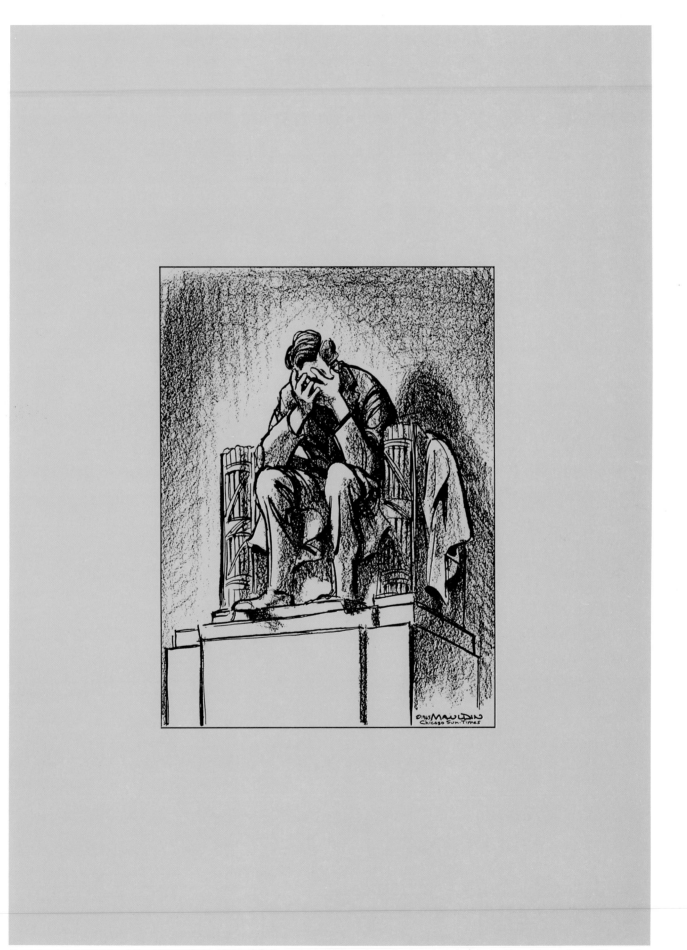

Cartoonist Bill Mauldin showed the memorial statue of Lincoln grieving for the slain President, John Kennedy.

RICHARD AVEDON

Mod model Twiggy in mad make-up.

The Great Put-on

If you are serious about fashion, you don't take it seriously.

MODEL PEGGY MOFFITT

One way the youth of the '60s showed their rebellion against convention was in the manner in which they dressed. On one day they might appear with their feet, legs, bosoms and behinds bare. The next day they would cover everything all up again, in gypsy skirts, billowing pants, boots, jewelry and scarves. Girls painted their eyes and paled their lips; both sexes let their hair grow long. Both sexes also wore pants and jackets of colorful velvet and lace.

Much of this was a gigantic put-on, a slam at all the classic little black dresses and sack suits of tradition, but to the astonishment and general dismay of more sedate citizens, what began as an in joke among young people kicked off a revolution both in fashions and in the way those fashions got started. For the first time, the style-setters were not an exclusive few designers and the elegant women who wore their clothes. Now, ideas for fashion came from the streets, and designers adjusted to them.

"What I do is watch what kids are putting together for themselves," said designer Rudi Gernreich. One thing that Gernreich saw was the tendency to wear less and show more. In 1964 he startled the country with a completely topless bathing suit — inspiring other designers to bare the other end *(right)*.

Another kid-watcher was Mary Quant in London, who observed with a magnificently mixed metaphor that "something in the air was coming to the boil" in the length of skirts. What was coming to a boil was the impulse to show more leg. In 1960, she began showing dresses that climbed above the knee. Skirts went up and up, until they became the miniskirt and ultimately the micro, with the shortest hemlines women had worn — and men gazed upon — in the whole history of civilized costume.

With great solemnity, historians and anthropologists analyzed the meaning of the wild, revealing clothes of the '60s. "Fashion is essentially a game of hide-and-seek between seduction and prudery," explained museum curator and costume historian James Laver. "We are going through a period of extreme exhibitionism," said anthropologist Margaret Mead. One ordinary, middle-aged American was a bit less scholarly. "It's as though you just got out of jail after fifteen years for sex offenses," he marveled, "and all your erotic fantasies are walking around."

A 1967 backless bathing suit hits a new low. Said "Vogue": "The cutout gives a certain deliciousness to the small of the back."

Partner of Mary Quant in spreading the miniskirt message was Twiggy, left, a teen-age sprig of a cockney whose real name was Lesley Hornby. Fragile, childish and impish, Twiggy, according to Mary Quant, was "the knockout beauty of our time." The skinny Twiggy acknowledged her role as the decade's leading model: "H'it's not really wot you'd call a figger," said she, "but with me funny face, me funny skirts and me funny accent somehow it all combined to work out just lovely." Twiggy made famous an entire look that included off-beat colors, fabrics and unexpected shapes. The look was called Mod and in one form or another it lasted the decade. By 1970 stockings appeared in every imaginable color and texture. Chains multiplied. And the skirt, adapted into American designs like the dress at right, stayed short, exposing all manner of female legs — including those of women who should have known better.

BARRY KAPLAN

Mod and Miniskirts

RONALD FITZGIBBON

RICHARD AVEDON

In the early '60s the teen-age world was suddenly hit by the rock-and-roll phenomenon of the Beatles, four long-haired Liverpool musicians (above) whose outrageous irreverence and appearance took youth everywhere by storm (page 60).

Rushing to imitate all aspects of the life style of their idols, young Americans stopped cutting their hair off and started adorning themselves in Edwardian shapes and wild colors. Their exuberant new style of dressing soon spread from Beatlemania to countrywide and worldwide popular fashion.

The Male of the Species

RAYMUNDO DE LARRAIN

RAYMUNDO DE LARRAIN

*In 1965 young people seeking
a past to cling to adopted czarist
Russia. An impetus was
"Doctor Zhivago," a popular movie
of a best-selling historical novel
by Soviet author Boris Pasternak.
The film was jammed with
actors wearing military boots, mid-
calf greatcoats, and fur hats
and stoles. American youth promptly
exaggerated this attire. Boots
reached the thighs, coat hems swept
the street, hats doubled in size;
and the Russian look became as all-
American as the miniskirt.*

Coexistence by Couturier

PENATI

RICHARD DAVIS   JAMES MOORE

In dress-up clothes, young men and women often seemed determined to look as though they lived any place and at any era except where they were—in the United States during the '60s. On these pages, from upper left, are some of the more romantic times and places they liked: Marco Polo's mysterious, beautiful Cathay; below it, India, in an age when maharajahs ruled their people in jeweled jackets; next, Romany, the never-never land of gay, colorful gypsies; and at upper right, Jane Austen's England of demurely dressed women and men in fancy high-collared coats. And, as the foursome at lower right indicate, any and all of these periods could blend with one another—and with hairstyles reminiscent of young squires of King Arthur's court.

RICHARD DAVIS

RICHARD DAVIS

Another Time and Place

Of all the highly bizarre fashions that appeared in the '60s, perhaps the most grotesque was the funky look. As explained by one earnest teenager, a funky ensemble was not something one went to a store and bought, but rather the result of "putting together things that don't go together, but go together— you know what I mean?" Before the clothes revolution, the word "funk" meant either very cowardly or depressed. Now it seemed to mean something quite extraordinary, such as wearing a fringed vest and bead necklace in place of a shirt or finding a draped pink wraparound blouse of the '40s in the attic and wearing it with 15 pieces of leather laced to make one pair of pants.

The Funky Fad

RAYMUNDO DE LARRAIN

One inevitable result of the trend toward nudity was the "see-through" costume. Although some brave youngsters put transparent clothes on bare bodies, most women who wore them preserved modesty by first covering themselves in skintight, flesh-colored undergarments called body stockings. Even with the compromise, however, not everyone favored the diminishing dress. "It won't go much beyond this, I hope," sighed designer Steven Brody. "I don't want to make G-strings."

Next to Nothing

KEN DUNCAN

114

FRANCO RUBARTELLI

Senior citizens on an outing in a Seal Beach, California, retirement town.

Sunset Village

One day in Des Moines at a board meeting, I realized I only knew half the people there and only knew half of them well. Went home and said to Mother, we may just as well go to California and a retirement town.

HAROLD HOLDEN, 76, SEAL BEACH LEISURE WORLD

These retirement villages are just an effort to throw us into a corner and forget us.

MAX FRIEDSON, 71, CONGRESS OF SENIOR CITIZENS

Although the attention of America seemed riveted on the generation under 30, at the other end of the life scale something almost as big was brewing. By mid-decade the number of people past 50 had reached 45 million. These oldsters had a problem: They were, said United Auto Workers head Walter Reuther, "too old to work and too young to die."

Many of the aging simply stayed put in their hometowns. Some entered nursing homes and old-age institutions. But a growing army of active elders started new lives built around a phenomenon of the '60s called "retirement towns," communities tailored exclusively for people over 50.

The first retirement town of its kind was opened in Arizona in 1960 by Del Webb, a daring builder and entrepreneur. He committed two million dollars and 30,000 acres northwest of Phoenix to the heretical idea that pleasant houses and recreation facilities, away from cities, children, grandchildren and cold weather, would have great appeal to old folks. The first weekend after his project opened, he sold 272 houses. By 1970 similar communities had sprung up in the resort states of Florida and California, in the Middle West, New England and on the East Coast.

In the houses and apartments of these retirement towns, residents found such conveniences as grab-bars in bathrooms and electric outlets raised three feet from the floor to save stooping. Medical centers were unobtrusively but carefully located right in the heart of the towns.

The towns did everything to banish the cares —and even the awareness—of age. Residents were referred to as adults, mature adults, or even empty-nesters—anything but old people. All the elements of a full life were easily accessible: the market, the golf course, the medical center, the ubiquitous clubhouses. At the latter, bulletin boards announced events ranging from Saturday night dances to "Lip Reading Class—for beginners, no fee, Wed. a.m., 10-12." And friends were near. "I was wild for companionship," said a 63-year-old woman. "Now all I have to do is stand on the patio and yell 'Coffee' and six people come running." In fact, in a typical retirement town like Seal Beach Leisure World in California, pictured in brochure style on the following pages, lively companionship was the strongest of all sales points.

Mrs. Fred Allen, 66,
tends calla lilies in the
garden of her Leisure World home.

"*Heck fire, it's like being on a vacation constantly.*" *So says a happy resident of Seal Beach Leisure World in sunny Southern California. For only $1,000 to $4,500—plus the modest monthly maintenance charge of from $92 to $127—some 12,000 mature adults (no "senior citizens" here!) find every facility for pleasure and cultural fun they never before had time to explore. There are potters' wheels for the potters, easels for the painters, diamond saws for the lapidary lovers. For the sports-minded, the nine-hole golf course is waiting, and the bowling green in the center of town is a focus of attention. But these and the many other lavish Leisure World facilities—the shuffleboard courts, billiard rooms, swimming pools—are only a convenience. They are for use if and when wanted. There is no regimentation, no forced participation in activities. If "I'm not a joiner" is your motto, then lounge the day away in the sunshine if you prefer. Leisure World offers you the carefree life adults have earned the right to enjoy.*

Whether the prescription is a warm, soothing whirlpool bath for arthritis, scales for TOPS, the Take Off Pounds Sensibly club, or for help when unexpected illness strikes, residents are guaranteed "family doctor" attention at Leisure World. Located at the heart of the community is a medical clinic approved by Medicare as a Home Care Agency with 19 doctors, 31 registered nurses and a full staff of graduate nurses' aides and technicians. A physician and registered nurse and an ambulance are on duty 24 hours a day for any emergency. The more seriously sick are removed quickly, comfortably to a hospital outside. At Leisure World the goal is total peace of mind.

A visit to a gala at Leisure World can tell the whole story! Here the social and personal rapport among residents might well stand as an example to youth. The Barber Shoppers, real harmony makers, sing out their own lyrics: "Tint your hair and keep it curled, and stalk your prey at Leisure World." A chorus line is proof of the sprightliness that enlivens this adult community. "No one has time for anything," complains the show director when trying to schedule rehearsals. "They're all too busy." Thus, the happy bustle of Leisure World means discovering oneself and others, sharing pleasures and activities, fully enriching the most gratifying years of one's life.

In Leisure World, the one key word is living. Here the close companionship that adults are unlikely to get elsewhere is rich and highly fulfilling. A grandfather chuckles: "I know a bachelor that the ladies are doin' everythin' for. But none of 'em's approaching me. Me, I'm perfectly happy and satisfied here. Mostly you find it's association with the fellas you cultivate. I told my daughters, as long as I can take care of myself, I wanna live here." Said a resident's son when his widower dad, 64, found a widow bride, 65, five months after arrival: "It was kind of a shock. But we're tickled for them both. They're like a couple of eighteen-year-olds." All of the younger visitors are constantly amazed by the activity of Leisure World, one of the most socially active cities in America. "Anything you want to do here, they've got it," is one way of putting it. Free from congestion, litter, deterioration or other unpleasant conditions of the modern age, here is where "it's happening." In short, with its compassionate companionship it's a wonderful world for him, her and together.

Media

Four-year-old boy with his electronic teacher, Hamden, Connecticut.

The Print Panic

Television threatens to engulf the written word like a blob from outer space. The decay of the written word, of which the Saturday Evening Post's death is a symbol, is surely a tragedy, and maybe not a very small tragedy either.

STEWART ALSOP, *NEWSWEEK*

As computers streamlined the business of teaching children to read and television supplied more and more of the day's news and looking up facts became associated with terms like "input/output console" and "information-retrieval," a great many Americans began to wonder what was happening to the printed page. Would all knowledge soon be coming to them on cathode ray tubes or from electronic print-outs? What would happen to pen and ink, and books and periodicals? According to one prophet of the '60s, they were doomed. "It is true," wrote Marshall McLuhan, director of the Centre for Culture and Technology at Toronto University, "that there is more material written and printed and read today than ever before, but there is also a new electric technology that threatens this ancient technology of literacy built on the phonetic alphabet." McLuhan believed that literacy was bound to be the loser and argued his case in two of the decade's most provocative books, *The Gutenberg Galaxy* and *Understanding Media (page 135).*

To some people McLuhan's ideas were holy writ; to others they were nonsense—it was pointed out that some forms of the printed word (books, for example) flourished during the decade. Nevertheless, there were enough casualties in the publishing world to suggest that his message might in part be true. At least 163 magazines died during the decade, including, almost unbelievably, the 148-year-old *Saturday Evening Post*, a periodical so entwined in American life that some sentimentalists were ready to declare it a national treasure. Nearly as high was the toll of newspapers. Though not all of them were old and famous, and though some of them may even have deserved to die, the passing of 160 dailies seemed akin to catastrophe.

The Boston *Traveler* was out of business, and so were the Houston *Press*, the Pittsburgh *Sun-Telegraph* and the San Francisco *News-Call-Bulletin*. Oregon's incorruptible Portland *Reporter* called it quits midway through an 18-part series on a controversial freeway that was slated to slash across some of the city's prime real estate. Gone too was the 77-year-old Indianapolis *Times*, once the winner of a Pulitzer Prize for exposing the nightriding Ku Klux Klan. And in Rochester, New York, the 116-

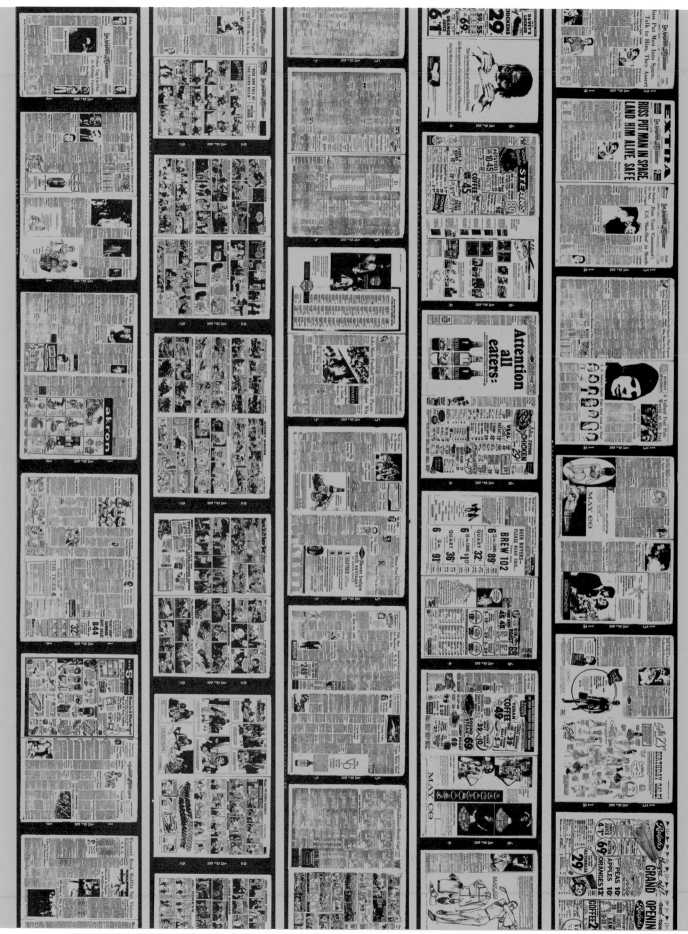

As of January 8, 1962, anyone who wanted to read the "Los Angeles Examiner" could do so only on microfilm; it had folded.

year-old *Abendpost*, one of the country's three German-language dailies, reluctantly published its own black-bordered obituary.

The owners of these papers almost never accused television of stealing readers, although sometimes TV was accused of beating the papers out of ads. And few publishers appeared to think that the printing press would succumb to the printed circuit. For what reason, otherwise, would publishers during the decade have started 176 *new* dailies? In their litany of complaints the culprit was always money. Papers merged or failed or ran into trouble because production costs had risen and the revenue from readers and ads did not keep pace, or because of labor troubles. In the five years between 1962 and 1967, strikes left New Yorkers without their accustomed papers for a total of 279 days. One Boston *Traveler* executive even claimed that a shortage of newsboys, traditionally low-paid, had helped to kill his paper, since the shortage had required the management to hire grown men at nine dollars a day.

At decade's end Boston was down from five daily papers to four (a century earlier Bostonians had had 120 periodicals to choose from), Detroit was down from three to two, and Los Angeles was also down to two. New York, the largest city in the land, suffered the gravest loss of all. It had started the 20th Century with 15 major papers, and the decade with seven; it ended with three. Although faithful readers could understand the economic logic behind the suspensions, it was not easy to accept the passing of papers they had been buying all their lives.

"I could cry, I could just cry," said one New York City secretary on the day the *World Journal Tribune* ceased publication, taking with it into oblivion a trio of familiar newspaper voices—and a whole journalistic tradition. The Wijit, as it was inevitably called, was a paper that almost no one knew; it lived just under nine months and died in what many thought of as a mercy killing. But its tripartite name repre-

Optimistic ads failed to stave off the death of the Wijit in 1967

132

sented three mastheads, all of which had existed separately only months before—the *World-Telegram and Sun*, the *Journal-American* and the *Herald Tribune*. Buried in its genealogy were 13 former New York City dailies, a few of them famous.

One of the WJT's ancestors was Joseph Pulitzer's pugnacious old *World*, brilliantly edited and brash enough to call President Teddy Roosevelt a liar. Another was William Randolph Hearst's flamboyant *Journal*, which started the craze for comic strips with a character called the "Yellow Kid" and also may have started the Spanish-American War with its inflammatory reporting of a Cuban rebellion. A third famous Wijit ancestor was James Gordon Bennett's sprightly *Herald*, which ordered its reporters to call "limbs" legs and "inexpressibles" pantaloons. Yet another, Horace Greeley's high-principled *Tribune*, fought for the abolition of slavery and hired Karl Marx to report on European politics, a job he held for 11 years, until Greeley, in a historic exploitation of the worker, cut his salary from $10 to $5 a week.

By the time the *Herald* and *Tribune* joined forces in 1924 they had long since established the journalistic tradition of good writing and reporting that stayed with the *Trib* to the end. Among the famous names on its roster were Henry James, the *Tribune's* man in Paris in 1875, and Mark Twain, who wrote an article for the *Herald*, in 1864, on a trip through Europe and the Holy Land with a group of fellow Americans. Twain's report roasted the behavior of his companions and later became the basis for his book *The Innocents Abroad*. It was the *Herald* that sent Stanley in search of Livingstone and assigned the dashing and romantic Richard Harding Davis to cover Great Britain's Boer War.

Separately or together, the two papers launched the careers of Robert Benchley and John O'Hara, and nourished the talents of Don Marquis and Grantland Rice and Red Smith. ("In nine minutes of actual combat today, Jack Dempsey crushed Jess Willard into a shapeless mass of gore and battered flesh," wrote Grantland Rice in his featured Sportlight column; and Red Smith, off on a skiing junket with a busload of amateurs, reported on "the long, hawklike swoop of an accomplished skier performing the graceful glockenspiel and then, at the instant when he seems certain to catapult into a pack of women and children at the foot of the slope, coming to a halt in a cloud of powdered snow as he executes a perfect schlemiel.")

Then, at 5 p.m. on a hot, sticky August afternoon, at the end of its second 114-day strike in three years, it was all over. On commuter trains and subways and buses the next morning, *Herald Tribune* readers went without the drama criticism of Walter Kerr and John Crosby's pungent commentary on the previous night's television. There was no Walter Lippmann or Joseph Alsop to guide their political thinking, no Art Buchwald to make the profound seem ridiculous. Never again would the morning begin with Clementine Paddleford's rhapsodies to food ("The waiter's spoon dips in and the soufflé responds with a rapturous sigh as it settles softly to melt and vanish in a moment like smoke in a dream"). And thereafter *Trib* regulars would have to look elsewhere for the trenchant movie reviews of Judith Crist and Tom Wolfe's excited but occasionally incomprehensible reports on the pop scene ("Bangs manes bouffants beehives Beatle caps," wrote Wolfe of a rock concert audience, "butter faces brush-on lashes decal eyes puffy sweaters French thrust bras flailing leather blue jeans stretch pants stretch jeans honeydew bottoms eclair shanks elf boots ballerinas Knight slippers, hundreds of them, these flaming little buds, bobbing and screaming, rocketing around inside the Academy of Music Theater underneath that vast old mouldering cherub dome up there—aren't they supermarvelous!"). The *Herald Tribune* and its ill-starred heir, the Wijit, were gone, along with 159 other daily papers, and the decade and the nation were the poorer.

A Multiplicity of Myths

As newspapers and magazines folded at an accelerating rate and the ghostly glow of television spread across the land, some pundits of the '60s suggested that the U.S. was turning into a nation of yahoos. One pundit who disagreed was a lean, tweedy Canadian scholar named Marshall McLuhan. Far from destroying our minds, said McLuhan, television and

Marshall McLuhan is surrounded by his own TV image.

the other new means of electronic communication were hatching one of the greatest revolutions ever to hit Western man.

According to McLuhan, the new media were re-ordering man's senses, weaning him from the age-old habit of collecting information from the printed page, conditioning him to be "tribal" again, to live "mythically and integrally." Like the "horizonless, boundless" world of primitive people around a campfire, the modern world was without boundaries. "Time has ceased," McLuhan said, "space has vanished. We now live in a *global* village . . . a simultaneous happening."

The author of this proclamation seemed an unlikely herald for a swiftly changing world. A professor of literature at Toronto University and a specialist in the works of Elizabethan author Thomas Nashe, McLuhan was the very model of the cloistered don. His office, according to pop-culture critic Tom Wolfe, looked like "the receiving bin of a secondhand bookstore," and he dressed in a negligent mélange of well-worn tweeds set off by a snap-on necktie.

But McLuhan was also in the know about the new, and had been ever since 1936, when, at the University of Wisconsin, he had come face to face with a freshman class he was unable to understand and had

"felt an urgent need to study their popular culture in order to get through." His first book on the subject, published in 1951, was a study of sex in advertising, *The Mechanical Bride.* It was followed in the '60s by the two books that made him famous, *The Gutenberg Galaxy: The Making of Typographic Man* (1962) and *Understanding Media: The Extensions of Man* (1964). In the first of these, McLuhan asserted that Johann Gutenberg's invention of movable type in the 15th Century had reoriented man and his environment. As McLuhan put it in one of the book's breathless chapter headings: "The invention of typography confirmed and extended the new visual stress of applied knowledge, providing the first uniformly repeatable *commodity*, the first assembly line, and the first mass-production."

Print expelled man from a warm, safe "tribal" existence in which he got his information by ear and propelled him into a cold, forbidding world in which he sat, silent and alone, reading and writing books. In addition, print made man *linear.* It addicted him to straight lines of all sorts, from straight-ahead, logical, step-by-step thinking to straight-up-the-corporate-ladder personal ambition.

But television, with its combination of picture and sound, was changing all that—and fast. It was accustoming man to be oral again and to receive ideas in the form of images. "A few decades hence," McLuhan prophesied, "it will be easy to describe the revolution in human perception and motivation that resulted from beholding the new mosaic mesh of the TV image. Today it is futile to discuss it."

Nevertheless, two years later he tried. And considering that *Understanding Media* sold 9,000 copies in hardcover and more than 100,000 in paperback, he succeeded. *Understanding Media* elaborated, adumbrated, orchestrated, repeated and inflated the central theme of the previous book: that the *way* people get information, rather than the information itself, is the key fact in history; or, in McLuhan's words, the *medium* is the message.

There was no denying that McLuhan was onto something important. The trouble was that his arguments skittered all over Western cultural history, connecting things and ideas never before connected. They were ingenious and unexpected—and they did not always make sense. As Dwight McDonald observed in his review of *Understanding Media*, "A single page is impressive, two are stimulating, five raise serious doubts, ten confirm them."

Some critics were disturbed by McLuhan's dizzying flights of logic—as for instance when he proved that man was abandoning his "linear" habits by citing the disappearance of production lines (Detroit would have been surprised), stag lines, reception lines, political party lines and the lines down the back of women's stockings. Other critics were upset by the light-hearted way McLuhan used facts. One authority on James Joyce claimed, for example, that McLuhan, in his free lifting of material from Joyce, seldom quoted correctly, and that in any case the material had little relevance to McLuhan's point.

Whether McLuhan was right or wrong, a gadfly or one of the century's seminal thinkers, no one could rival him as a purveyor of up-to-date prophesies and explanations for everything under the sun. As the accompanying excerpts from his book *Understanding Media* show, McLuhan knew why fishnet stockings were in fashion, the real reason the Brooklyn Dodgers had moved to Los Angeles and what lay behind the American liking for big cars. He was the decade's all-purpose answer man. And the answers were all —or almost all—relayed through the printed word.

ON SPORTS: *The removal of the Brooklyn Dodgers to Los Angeles was a portent in itself. Baseball moved West in an attempt to retain an audience after TV struck. The characteristic mode of the baseball game is that it features one-thing-at-a-time. . . . With the advent of TV, such isolation of the individual performance as occurs in baseball became unacceptable. Interest in baseball declined.*

ON CLOTHES AND STYLES: *Clothing and styling in the past decade have gone so tactile and sculptural that they present a sort of exaggerated evidence of the new qualities of the TV mosaic. The TV extension of our nerves in hirsute pattern possesses the power to evoke a flood of related imagery in clothing, hairdo, walk, and gesture.*

ON FISHNET STOCKINGS: *The open-mesh silk stocking is far more sensuous than the smooth nylon, just because the eye must act as hand in filling in and completing the image, exactly as in the mosaic of the TV image.*

ON AMERICAN CARS: *The American car had been fashioned in accordance with the VISUAL mandates of the typographic and movie images. The American car was an enclosed space, not a tactile space. And an enclosed space is one in which all spacial qualities have been reduced to visual terms. So in the American car, as the French observed decades ago, "one is not on the road, one is in the car."*

Black Emergence

Marching to Montgomery, Alabama, during a voter registration drive, 1965

A New Kind of Image

There has been a re-evaluation of our slave philosophy that permitted us to be satisfied with the leftovers at the back door rather than demand a full serving at the family dinner table.

AARON HENRY, PRESIDENT OF THE MISSISSIPPI NAACP

In 1963, when the picture at right was taken in Birmingham, Alabama, most of the 11 million Negroes in the South were deprived—through poll taxes and trumped-up literacy tests—of their Constitutional right to vote. In North and South alike, black children were still confined to segregated schools that usually prepared them for only the most menial jobs.

But as the '60s got underway, the nation's 19 million Negro Americans served notice that they would endure these circumstances no longer. Their dramatic emergence was activated in a massive two-phased movement, the first a crusade of nonviolence, the second a campaign of militancy. The nonviolent phase was conducted under the leadership of an Alabama preacher, Dr. Martin Luther King Jr., who guided Southern blacks on a series of sit-ins and protest marches. And though he was jailed, roughed up and stabbed before finally being assassinated by a white ex-convict *(page 95)*, he never during his life abandoned the course of nonviolent protest.

The leaders of the second phase were of a totally different persuasion. They were tough, angry men who advocated physical violence in speech and writing and who did not hesitate to join directly in the battle. Together with King, they went a long way toward changing the black man's world. By 1970, as just one consequence of having won the vote, 1,500 Negroes held elective office, from Massachusetts' Senator Edward W. Brooke to hundreds of state legislators, judges and school board officials. Educational opportunities had improved; black enrollment at Cornell University, for instance, was 300 in the fall of 1969, up from a few dozen five years before. Economic opportunity was opening up in previously all-white territory. In 1966, for example, the Boston Celtics pro basketball team became the first major league sports club to put a Negro in management when they paid star center Bill Russell more than $200,000 to coach their world championship team.

At decade's end, there was still far too much inequity (29 per cent of the Negro population still lived below the poverty level versus 8 per cent for whites), but black Americans had formed a proud new image of themselves—perhaps the decade's major advance. Mrs. Ethel Mae Pettway of Gee's Bend, Alabama, summed it up in 1970: "We're not ashamed anymore."

A fire hose batters blacks on a wall in Birmingham, Alabama, where the first real gains of the decade were made in civil rights.

When the civil rights movement began, Selma, Alabama, had voting rolls that were 99 per cent white, a figure that triggered dramatic demonstrations and led the satirist Art Buchwald to write the fantasy excerpted here.

"Fine, George, fine. Ah'd be glad to register you as soon as you answer a few of these here questions," the registrar says. "Now, first off, what is your education?"

Under the eyes of white officials, blacks register in the South.

"I was a Rhodes scholar, received a B.A. from Columbia, a masters from Harvard, a Ph.D. from MIT."

"That's just fine, George. Now would you please read somethin' from this here newspaper?"

"It's in Chinese."

"That's right."

George reads from the Chinese paper. The registrar is thrown, but he doesn't want to show it. He goes to his safe and takes out a clay jar. "George, would you be so kind to read for me any two of these Dead Sea Scrolls?"

George reads but stumbles on a word.

"Ah'm sorry, George. You've failed the literacy test, but you can come back next year and try again."

As George leaves the office, a white Alabaman comes in to register to vote.

The registrar says to him, "Would you please spell cat for me?" SON OF THE GREAT SOCIETY BY ART BUCHWALD

Bearing a huge American flag, black youths lead a rally through Selma, urging the brothers and sisters to get out and vote.

141

White college students picket in Washington, D.C., in 1960.

We shall overcome, we shall overcome,
We shall overcome someday.
Oh, deep in my heart, I do believe
We shall overcome someday.
We'll walk hand in hand,
We'll walk hand in hand,
We'll walk hand in hand someday.
Oh, deep in my heart, I do believe
We shall overcome someday.

"WE SHALL OVERCOME" BY ZILPHIA HORTON,
FRANK HAMILTON, GUY CARAWAN, PETE SEEGER
TRO- ©Copyright 1960 & 1963 LUDLOW MUSIC, INC. New York. Used by permission.

Black and white Americans join hands at the White House in 1965 to sing the anthem of nonviolence, "We Shall Overcome."

Framed by the flag, Dr. King expounds on his dream.

In August 1963, some 200,000 persons marched on Washington to demonstrate for civil rights. The climax was this moving plea.

I have a dream that one day this nation will rise up, live out the true meaning of its creed: "We hold these truths to be self-evident, that all men are created equal." I have a dream that one day on the red hills of Georgia sons of former slaves and the sons of former slave-owners will be able to sit down together at the table of brotherhood. I have a dream that one day even the state of Mississippi, a state sweltering with the heat of injustice . . . will be transformed into an oasis of freedom and justice. I have a dream that my four little children will one day live in a nation where they will not be judged by the color of their skin but by the content of their character. MARTIN LUTHER KING JR.

When the marchers assembled, they covered the ground from the Lincoln Memorial to the Washington Monument (rear).

With Alabama divided over voting rights, Governor Wallace meets with President Johnson and the press in Washington.

When the blacks began to push for civil rights
early in the decade, many Americans
reacted with irritation and even with rage. One of
the chief spokesmen for Southern racism
was the Governor of Alabama, George Wallace, some
of whose convictions are recorded below.

I draw the line in the dust and toss the gauntlet before
the feet of tyranny and I say segregation now, segregation tomorrow, segregation forever.

INAUGURAL ADDRESS, JANUARY 14, 1963

I see no need for any legislation. The legislation and
the laws are already on the books.

PRESS CONFERENCE IN WASHINGTON, MARCH 13, 1965

Regardless of what the national news media say about
me and my administration, we have done the best we
could to help all the people of our state. Yet in some
places groups are doing everything that they can to
provoke.

ADDRESS TO ALABAMA EDUCATION ASSOCIATION, MARCH 1965

The Civil Rights Law is such that any grievance can
be settled in court, and demonstrations haven't one
thing to do with it. . . . The Negro has no more griev-
ances here than in any other state. Why, Martin
Luther King said himself that Chicago is the most segregated city in the country.

INTERVIEW WITH THE CHRISTIAN SCIENCE MONITOR, MARCH 15, 1965

If we, of course, were stampeded into doing away with
all policemen who have been charged with police bru-
tality, there wouldn't be hardly enough policemen in
the United States today to even have traffic control.

ON FACE THE NATION, CBS-TV, MARCH 14, 1965

Cities and Spirits Inflamed

Between 1964 and 1967, black frustration at the gap between promise and performance in civil rights reached the flash point, and 58 cities exploded in riots that left 141 persons dead and 4,552 injured. These riots were generally spontaneous eruptions that began when minor incidents between police and blacks blew up into urban warfare; the result was shocking damage to life and property. In Watts, the black ghetto of Los Angeles, and in Newark, the fracases began initially over tickets for traffic violations. In Detroit *(right)*, a routine raid on a black speakeasy drew a crowd that was curious at first, then angry and out of control; the result was the worst race riot of the decade, with a toll of 42 dead and 386 injured after nine days of fire and looting.

The white man don't like nothing black but a Cadillac. We must wage guerrilla war on these honkies.

H. RAP BROWN

You've got to make a man proud of the fact he's black, make him want to fight for it. Putting Weaver in the Cabinet or paying Willie Mays $100,000 a year just doesn't do it. You've got to show him Whitey can be SCARED of him.

DAN WATTS, EDITOR, *LIBERATOR* MAGAZINE

Those buildings going up was a pretty sight. I sat right here and watched them go. And there wasn't nothing them honkies could do but sweat to put it out.

DETROIT RIOTER

Well, you can say regret and then you can say there are some who are glad it happened. Now, me personally, I feel that I regret it, yes. But, deep down inside I know I was feeling some joy while it was going on, simply because I am a Negro. WATTS COLLEGE STUDENT

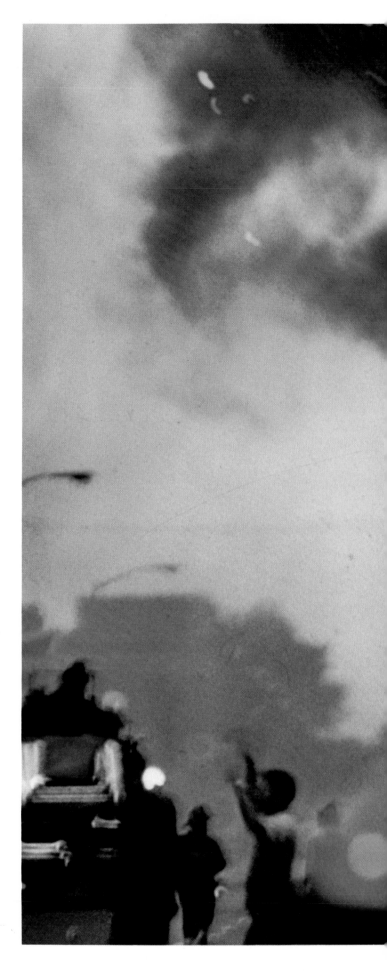

Orange flames lick the sky as $44 million worth of property in Detroit crumbles during the long, hot summer of 1967.

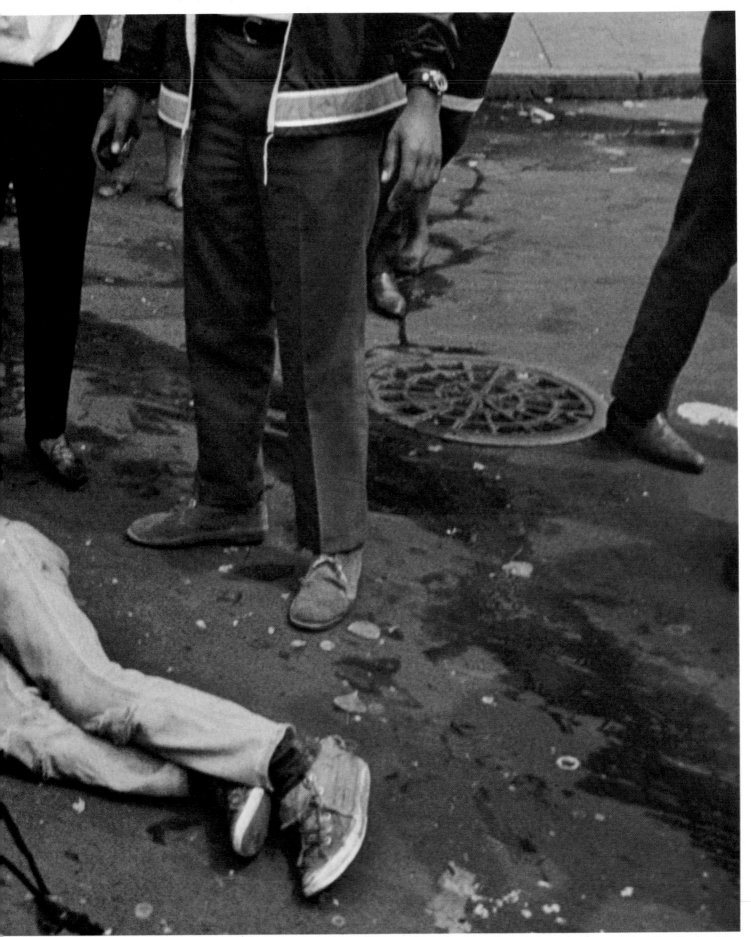

During a 1967 riot in Newark, New Jersey, a wounded child lies in a pool of his own blood as a police officer bends over him.

Almost hidden by hard-eyed, neatly dressed bodyguards, Elijah Muhammad (rear, in jeweled fez) addresses Black Muslims.

Angry Voices Speak Out

While Martin Luther King Jr. was continuing to advocate nonviolence, other blacks were making it clear they were ready to fight for their rights. One of the first to throw down the militant challenge was Elijah Muhammad *(left)*, a 120-pound wisp of a man who claimed he had encountered "Allah on earth" and been designated "messenger" for the doctrine of black supremacy. As preached by Elijah to a sect called the Black Muslims, that doctrine forbade its members to drink, smoke, use dope, chase women or do anything else reminiscent of the simple-minded darkie stereotype. Elijah's teachings, though they were sprinkled with the mythology and metaphor common to any religious sect, nevertheless had a strong appeal for emerging blacks; and they became the progenitors of the concepts of black power and black nationalism and the belief that black is beautiful. Some excerpts from Elijah's preachings appear below. On the following pages are samplings of other spokesmen of the new generation of black militants.

Black Man, not White Man, was Original Man.

Negroes must take over for themselves lands, property and civilization.

When a Negro marries a white, the children are usually spotted. Blackbirds mate with their own kind. Blackbirds do not mate with red or orange birds. We do not want spotted children.

Get away from the white man. Get away from the white man's religion of Christianity. Stand up and fight. Do the same by them as they do by you. You have no right to fear white people if you know the truth.

MALCOLM X

Malcolm X, one of the earliest to urge his people to be proud of being black, was killed in 1965. Below are excerpts from his speeches.

The day of nonviolent resistance is over. The next thing you'll see here in America—and please don't blame it on me when you see it—you will see the same things that have taken place among other people on this earth whose condition was parallel to the 22 million Afro-Americans in this country.

TO THE MILITANT LABOR FORUM, MAY 1964

It was stones yesterday, Molotov cocktails today; it will be hand grenades tomorrow and whatever else is available the next day. You should not feel that I am inciting someone to violence. I'm only warning of a powder keg situation. You can take it or leave it.

TO THE MILITANT LABOR FORUM, APRIL 1964

If they make the Ku Klux Klan nonviolent, I'll be nonviolent. If they make the White Citizens Council nonviolent, I'll be nonviolent. But as long as you've got somebody else not being nonviolent, I don't want anybody coming to me talking any nonviolent talk.

TO MISSISSIPPI YOUTH, DECEMBER 1964

We nationalists used to think we were militant. We were just dogmatic. It didn't bring us anything. Now I know it's smarter to say you're going to shoot a man for what he is doing to you than because he is white. If you attack him because he is white, you give him no out. He can't stop being white. We've got to give the man a chance. He probably won't take it, the snake. But we've got to give him a chance.

TO THE ORGANIZATION OF AFRO-AMERICAN UNITY, EARLY 1965

Stokely Carmichael, one-time chairman of the Student Nonviolent Coordinating Committee, coined the phrase "black power."

Black power means black people coming together to form a political force and either electing representatives or forcing their representatives to speak their needs. It's an economic and physical block that can exercise its strength in the black community instead of letting the job go to the Democratic or Republican parties or a white-controlled black man set up as a puppet to represent black people. WE pick the brother and make sure he fulfills OUR needs. Black power doesn't mean anti-white, violence, separatism or any other racist things the press says it means. It's saying, "Look, buddy, we're not laying a vote on you unless you lay so many schools, hospitals, playgrounds and jobs on us."

INTERVIEW WITH *LIFE* PHOTOGRAPHER GORDON PARKS, 1967

Integration today means the man who "makes it," leaving his black brothers behind in the ghetto as fast as his new sports car will take him. It has no relevance to the Harlem wino or to the cottonpicker making $3 a day. As a lady I know once said, "The food that Ralph Bunche eats doesn't fill my stomach.". . .

No one ever talked about "white power" because power in this country IS white. . . . The furor over that black panther reveals the problems that white America has with color and sex; the furor over "black power" reveals how deep racism runs and the great fear which is attached to it.

FROM *THE NEW YORK REVIEW OF BOOKS,* SEPTEMBER 22, 1966

STOKELY CARMICHAEL

LE ROI JONES

Playwright LeRoi Jones led the United Black Brothers in a strident voter registration campaign that put the blacks in control of Newark.

I'm in favor of black people taking power by the quickest, easiest, most successful means they can employ. Malcolm X said the ballot or the bullet. Newark is a particular situation where the ballot seems to be most advantageous. I believe we have to survive. I didn't invent slavery; I didn't invent the white man. What we're trying to do is deal with him in the best way we can.

INTERVIEW IN *THE WASHINGTON POST*, APRIL 1968

How can anybody live in this world without seeing what's going on? We began as slaves and have never existed to the man as human beings with rights equal to his. During the rebellions here in Newark, Negroes who were looking out the windows were shot because they were black. Negroes who believe they can slip into the white man's society are badly mistaken. The only established Negro leadership reflects white attitudes, urging patience after 350 years of patience. These leaders have the money, which whites are all too eager to give, to keep us down. And that represents power. Now they're going to have to be our own leaders.

INTERVIEW WITH *LIFE*, DECEMBER 1968

Blacks have to fashion a world where they can live with dignity and restraint. I am not interested in being a murderer, but then I'm not interested in being a dier, either. I'm not going to kill you, but I'm not going to let you kill me. Last summer they were shooting us down in the streets.

PRESS CONFERENCE IN NEWARK, APRIL 1968

Eldridge Cleaver won fame through his best-selling book, "Soul on Ice," excerpted below. He wrote it in California's Folsom State Prison.

I have, so to speak, washed my hands in the blood of the martyr, Malcolm X. I have tried a tentative compromise by adopting a select vocabulary, so that now when I see the whites of THEIR eyes, instead of saying "devil" or "beast" I say "imperialist" or "colonialist," and everyone seems to be happier....

One device evolved by the whites was to tab whatever the blacks did with the prefix "Negro." We had NEGRO literature, NEGRO athletes, NEGRO music, NEGRO doctors, NEGRO politicians, NEGRO workers. The malignant ingeniousness of this device is that although it accurately describes an objective biological fact—or at least, a sociological fact in America—it concealed the paramount psychological fact: that to the white mind, prefixing anything with "Negro" automatically consigned it to an inferior category.

FROM *SOUL ON ICE*

We've had "Pig Power" in this country and even white people are now becoming victims of Pig Power. And in fact we need a coalition of White Power and every other hue of power in order to rebuke the pigs and bring them back in their place....

It's necessary for people to take a revolutionary position against everything that exists on the planet earth today. Especially if you're black. You can't wait for them to call you up to bat. You just step up there and say, "I want to bat, sumbitch."

INTERVIEW IN *LOOK*, JANUARY 7, 1969

ELDRIDGE CLEAVER

Heritage and Humor

One of the dramatic aspects of the black social revolution of the '60s was the new stance of black Americans with respect to their self-image. "They have seized on their blackness and rallied around it," said militant leader Eldridge Cleaver. Much of the burgeoning black pride manifested itself in looking beyond a history of slavery for ethnic identity and finding it in Africa — in Africa's ancient kingdoms and newly emerging nations, and in African arts and sciences. Many black Americans began to wear African clothing, jewelry and hair styles, and to decorate their homes with African painting and sculpture. Some called themselves Afro-Americans and even returned to African religions.

Another clear manifestation of the change came from the quips and stories of the many black stand-up comedians who rose to national prominence during the decade. The techniques of these emerging stars varied. Some of them, like Dick Gregory, were openly angry; others, among them Flip Wilson and Godfrey Cambridge, covered their barbs with deceptive sugar-coating. But all of them asserted their self-pride and used humor to challenge existing social structures. "Sometimes people hate to be shown things but in the long run, they appreciate it," said old-timer Red Foxx. Like the sense of cultural identity, the new black comedy was a demand that white America accept black America on its own terms.

It is time to stop being ashamed of being black — time to stop trying to be white. When you see your daughter playing in the fields, with her nappy hair, her wide nose and her thick lips, tell her she is beautiful. TELL YOUR DAUGHTER SHE IS BEAUTIFUL.

STOKELY CARMICHAEL

Say it loud — I'm black and I'm proud.

SINGER JAMES BROWN

Wearing her hair African style and draped in an African robe, a girl of the '60s personifies the slogan Black is Beautiful.

Adorned in African robes and beating African drums, members of a Harlem Yoruba sect conduct a bembe, or religious service.

The search for African cultural roots strongly urged
by such leaders as Malcolm X and Floyd
McKissick (below), led some black Americans to the
ancient Yoruba religion of Nigeria,
a worship of nature gods and ancestral spirits.

*I believe that a psychological, cultural, philosophical
migration back to Africa will solve our problems. Not
a physical migration, but a cultural, psychological,
philosophical migration back to Africa—which means
restoring our common bond—will give us the spiritual strength and the incentive to strengthen our
political and social and economic position right here
in America, and to fight for the things that are ours by
right on this continent.* MALCOLM X

*The emergence of strong, independent black nations
in Africa has given great psychological impetus to
black nationalism in America. Black children and
adults now have a "homeland" of which to be proud.
The disgraceful American anti-black, anti-African
propaganda exemplified by the Tarzan books and movies is no longer believed. Black people are beginning
to rediscover their heritage and to be proud of it. . . .
Negro history, art, music and other aspects of
black culture make black people aware of their con-
tributions to the American heritage and to world
civilization.* FLOYD MCKISSICK

*We are sons and daughters of the most ancient soci-
eties on this planet.* LE ROI JONES

FLIP WILSON

*A satirist with a comic reverse twist, Wilson
performed on the black vaudeville "chitlin' circuit"
before hitting network TV and nightclubs.*

We got to do something about the Indians. The Indians aren't ready yet. Do you want to build a $50,000 home and have some guy put a wigwam next to it? I'm not against Indians. I tried to help an Indian once. He didn't appreciate it. I said to him, you Indians got a rough deal. If you guys'd think for a minute, you'da realized what was happening when the Pilgrims ran that Thanksgiving game on you. You remember that "Come over to dinner" thing? They never invited you back, did they? He said, "They NEVER invited you people." Now, I don't have to take this from a damn Indian. If I let him get away with this, next he'll want to marry my sister. I said Henry, why should they invite us to dinner when we're doing the cooking?

DICK GREGORY

*A pioneer of the new black comedy, Gregory often
lectured at colleges where he applied
his bitter irony to the crusade for black rights.*

I waited around till the lunch counter finally integrated . . . and then they didn't have what I wanted. (1961) In the early days when the British was the police, a white boy by the name of Paul Revere rode through the white community and said, "Get a gun, white folks. The police is coming." Now, you can understand the White Panthers. But the Black Panthers make you forget about your history, don't they? You got nerve enough to get upset over the riots when a nigger steal a television set and take it home with him, but you still give me that white boy history book telling me how your white folks got on that foreign ship and threw all that man's tea in the water. What the hell you mad at? That we got sense enough to take it home? (1969)

NIPSEY RUSSELL

A 25-year veteran of vaudeville and the nightclubs of Harlem's 125th Street, Russell blended song and dance routines with his ironic comedy.

How come there are so few Negroes on television? We can't get on, that's how come. We can't even get into the commercials—and I KNOW we have bad breath and dandruff. And how come there are no black brothers in the space program? I saw a picture of the space cadets and there wasn't a single soul brother. Not a black astronaut among them. They claim it's because they can't put ham hocks in that little tube they use. They say we'll want to ride around with the top down and we'll play the radio too loud. They say we'd want to paint the rocket chartreuse and wear silk mohair space suits. I had a cousin who washed out of the space program because instead of firing the reentry rockets, he kept zooming around hollering "One more time!"

JIMMY WALKER

Representing the next generation of black comics, this young New Yorker focused his humor almost entirely on the realities of ghetto life.

Where I come from there's a lot of black folks. I don't know if you're gonna believe that. And there are lots of robberies. What's been happening is black people been robbing black people. We robbin' us. Don't rob us. We ain't got nothin'. This brings me to the area of non-violent crime. Now in violent crime, we doin' damn good. But non-violent crime, I mean, when was the last time you saw a black investor or a black man gettin' busted for jugglin' the bank books? Just once I'd like to walk down 125th Street and have a black brother lay a counterfeit dollar on me. With a picture of Booker T. on it. I always say, what's the point of having a black brother in the Supreme Court if we don't commit crimes classy enough to get there?

Perhaps the most versatile of the black comics of the '60s was Godfrey Cambridge, who convulsed audiences with routines such as the one below, on the sly techniques a black man must use to get a taxi driven by a white. In addition, Cambridge devised the satirical game, "50 Easy Steps to the White House, a Great New Game for Discriminating People of All Races."

THE TRY AND LOOK INNOCENT METHOD: *I stand there, with a big broad smile on my face. I remove my sunglasses so no one thinks I'm a drug addict. I try to show I'm a white Negro, carrying my attache case. I hail them with the case. They think I'm an executive.*

THE SCREAMING-FRIENDLY APPROACH: *I scream, "GOING DOWNTOWN. DOWN. TOWN. I'M NOT GOING TO HARLEM!"*

THE TALKING OUT LOUD TO COMPANION METHOD: *I say, "No, I won't go to Harlem. Where do you live? The East Side? Good. I'll take you home." The driver overhears this. We jump in and I say "Park WEST Village."*

THE CATCH A COLD BUT GET HOME GAMBIT: *I wear a tuxedo and a boiled front shirt, I open my jacket. "See, tuxedo, boiled shirt." It's obvious no one sticks you up in a tuxedo. It works, but it can give you a hell of a cold.*

THE MONEY IN THE HAND ROUTINE: *I wave a $20 bill. At the same time I wave a dollar bill in the other hand to show I have change. If all these methods fail, I have another one up my sleeve—the Godfrey Cambridge Rent-A-White Service. You rent a white person for $2 an hour and all he has to do is hail cabs for you.*

YOU'RE ON YOUR WAY

24

MAKING IT

25 You are sent on a fact-finding mission for the CIA to Africa.

26 Become vice president of a bank after 15 years as a guard. Split immediately to Grosse Point.

27 Hire a W.A.S.P. chauffeur to drive your kids to school. Back to Philadelphia for ghetto lessons.

Your name appeared in too many ads. Lose one turn.	23	You give up karate lessons. Move to Westport.
3 dinners in a row with Roy Wilkins. Take a cab to Park Avenue.	22	You refuse the Nobel Prize, you are ungrateful. Go back to 13 and reconsider position.
You were seen lunching with Stokely. Go to jail.	21	John Birchers endorse you. Advance to 26.
You write a letter to the editor attacking air pollution and smog.	20	You incite a riot. Go to jail.
Shift to militant.	19	Shift to moderate.
Your peaceful demonstration led to violence. Go to jail.	18	Your book on black power wins Nobel Peace Prize. Go on the Tonight Show.
You are invited to White House dinner. Advance to 25.	17	For pasting black power posters in White House john, you lose two turns.
You are caught reading muslim paper. Go back to 13 and become militant.	16	You tear off tag on mattress in spite of warning.
You're on the cover of Time. Go on television via Africa.	15	You urge patience and restraint. Lose two turns.
You don't beat your wife, drink or smoke.	14	You don't beat your wife, drink or smoke.

WHERE IT'S AT

MODERATE **MILITANT**

LEAST RESISTANCE.

CHOOSE YOUR PATH OF

13

YOU MUST STOP HERE

12 You promote a Honky porter to file clerk. Advance to 13 and roll again.

11 You fire your Caucasian servant. Go back to Detroit

39

30	TONIGHT SHOW
31	MEET THE PRESS
32	You have a charge account at Tiffany's. That's going too far. Lose two turns.
33	GROSSE POINT
34	Your son intermarries, go to Africa in search of your roots (identity). Lose two turns.
35	You produce a movie "Flora & Fauna of Antarctica." Advance to 44.
36	You hire a Jewish lawyer, Puerto Rican houseboy, Polish nurse, Italian accountant and Irish press agent. You are a wonderful person, a tower of strength! Roll again.
37	You made a "U" turn Go to Jail You are as gentle as a rose.
38	PARK AVENUE

AFRICA Roll die for next turn. If odd—go to 30, If even—go to 31

JAIL To get out—roll an even number and go to 13

40 BEVERLY HILLS

41 Serve fried chicken, watermelon, chitterlings and black-eyed peas at Beverly Hills dinner party, you happy primitive you.

42 Run for mayor, you lose. Too pushy Skip one turn.

43 You run for mayor and win assuring people you will not be a "Negro" mayor. Roll again.

44 You win an Oscar, be grateful and "shake" Liz Taylor's hand on accepting award.

45 You're not invited to Harry Belafonte's Christmas party. Put him down on the Tonight Show.

46 You win presidential nomination. Do not demand a recount.

47 You refuse the Oscar. Tell your friends why on Park Avenue.

48 Vacation in Palm Beach without National Guard protection.

49 Choose George Wallace as your running mate. Justify t on Meet the Press

INSTRUCTIONS
THE GOAL: To get from the Ghetto to the White House · PLAYERS: 2, 3, or 4 / HOW TO PLAY: Roll die for moves. You must stop at 13 and make a decision to be a moderate or militant · All other instructions are on the board

50 THE WHITE HOUSE

GO, MAN

WATTS

HARLEM

MISSISSIPPI

NEWARK

THE WAY IT IS

	Ride to 13.
8	PHILADELPHIA
7	You try to organize welfare recipients. Back to Gorman
6	GARY, INDIANA
5	You refuse to break up your family so no welfare. Back to Gorman
4	You're in the Union! Advance to 13.
3	While waiting on union line police [...] you for loitering. Lose one turn.
2	Sorry! The apartment is rented.
1	DETROIT

Faces

Julie Nixon and David Eisenhower in Amherst, Massachusetts.

A Kaleidoscope of Celebrities

I think the only thing people are interested in is people. I think it's a starstruck nation.

DIANA VREELAND, EDITOR OF VOGUE

The creation of celebrities has always been a favorite American pastime; but in the go-go, multi-media world of the 1960s, bevies of newly famous faces flickered in and out of the public eye like the kaleidoscope of colors in a psychedelic light show. Never before had these public visages seemed so familiar; through magazines, newspapers and especially via the television camera, they entered virtually every living room in the country. "The televised image can become as real to the housewife as her husband, and much more attractive," wrote Joe McGinniss in *The Selling of the President 1968*, which told how Presidential candidate Richard Nixon used TV to bring his image home to the voters.

Not all the decade's personages were happy that their faces—and lives—had become public property. Julie Nixon and David Eisenhower, two college kids who happened to have been born into Presidential families, were frankly bewildered by the hubbub that attended their marriage in 1968. Other notables, such as convicted swindler Billie Sol Estes, would clearly have preferred total anonymity.

But most celebrities were delighted with their fame. Baby Jane Holzer, a dilettante fashion model, fairly basked in her role as leading jet-setter of 1964, even though her fame was largely the creation of a few bedazzled society columnists. Some celebrities even hired their own press agents to get their names in the papers. For others, particularly in the fields of arts and letters, the drumfire of publicity had a solid economic purpose. A number of authors in the stable of book publisher Bernard Geis, some with admittedly meager literary gifts, made fortunes in royalties as a result of massive promotion campaigns. "We promoted her just like a Hollywood starlet," said one of Geis's top assistants about sex novelist Jacqueline Susann. "Every conceivable angle was mined, so that the story was unending." And one of the decade's most bizarre personalities, a silver-haired leprechaun named Andy Warhol, helped foment a pop-art revolution by combining an unfailing knack for do-it-yourself press agentry with a modest talent for painting Campbell's soup cans. "Andy," said a close associate, as the price of Warhol's short-order masterpieces soared as high as $50,000, "is a promoter who creates—and his greatest creation is himself."

Lyndon Johnson and Vice President Hubert Humphrey strike a cheery back-at-the-ranch pose at the LBJ spread in Texas.

In 1967 a couple of amiable nightclub comedians, DAN ROWAN (left) and DICK MARTIN—one an ex-bartender, the other a former used-car dealer—put together the brightest, wackiest new show on TV. Called "Laugh-In," it was stitched together from snippets of video tape (some only an eighth of a second long) and comprised perhaps 350 sight gags, skits and one-liners. In the first 12 weeks of its hilarious life, "Laugh-In" climbed to fourth place in the ratings and at the end of the first season, it received the handsome total of four separate awards for television excellence.

Hollywood's sex symbol of the 1960s was RAQUEL WELCH, whose eye-boggling measurements (37-22-35) were very nearly matched by her awesome inability to act. No matter. She became an instant star on the strength of an appearance in the movie "One Million Years B.C." Playing the part of a Stone Age maiden, Raquel delivered four cryptic lines, the most memorable of which was "Ur-Loana-gunkl-Tumak." These grunts, and her costume—a tattered wolfskin bikini—endeared her to a generation. After 15 similar films, Raquel got a role that she, a still-aspiring actress, cherished, but that her real fans judged to be totally unsuited to her talents: the lead in the movie "Myra Breckinridge," during part of which she plays a man.

In 1964, SUSAN SONTAG, a beautiful, brainy young writer and college teacher, turned out for the "Partisan Review" a highbrow essay, "Notes on Camp," that catapulted both the author and her underground subject into national prominence. "Camp," said Miss Sontag, was "a vision of the world in terms of style." Its hallmarks were extravagance, artifice, a love of the unnatural. Camp was categorized as high, low or middle, and as unintentional or deliberate. Virginia Woolf's novel "Orlando," for example, was high camp; Batman comics were low; Lana Turner's acting was unintentional camp, Barbra Streisand's was deliberate. "Vogue" hailed Miss Sontag as "one of the most celebrated intellectuals in America," and "Life" called her "the most serious young writer we have." Whereupon, fed up with all the fuss over her essay and professing to be sorry she ever mentioned the subject of camp, she went off to write a novel.

When supper-club songstress DIAHANN CARROLL *starred on Broadway in "No Strings," Richard Rogers' show about a romance between a well-brought-up, middle-class Negro model and a white novelist, drama critic Walter Kerr was completely dazzled. "A girl with a sweet smile, brilliant dark eyes and a profile regal enough to belong on a coin," he said of her and went on to call her the "nicest thing" in the show. From stage-model, Miss Carroll proceeded to become a real model for "Harpers' Bazaar" and "Life" (below). Then she topped off her successes of the decade by winning the title role in "Julia," the first TV situation comedy to star a Negro.*

▼

For JAMES MEREDITH *the decade began on October 1, 1962, with his history-making enrollment in the previously all-white University of Mississippi, an act that triggered campus rioting and the call-up of 13,500 federal troops. In 1966 his one-man protest march, from Memphis to Jackson, Mississippi, was stopped when he was wounded by a shotgun blast. But near decade's end, civil rights martyr Meredith alienated many of his admirers, first by launching an abortive campaign for the seat of the popular Harlem Congressman Adam Clayton Powell and then by landing in jail as a landlord convicted of "harassing tenants."*

▶

Of the multiple problems faced during the decade by New York's lean and handsome Republican Mayor JOHN LINDSAY *(a transit strike, teachers' strikes, riots on campuses and in ghettos—to mention a few of the minor ones) none was more unrelenting than the problem of keeping New York clean. A field study by the high-domed Rand Corporation*

▼

and even help from the mayor himself scarcely made a dent in the problem. In fact, the electorate made garbage one of the main issues in Lindsay's 1969 reelection campaign. Though Lindsay failed to solve the crisis and in addition was repudiated by his own party, he won the election by 160,000 votes, mainly on the strength of his great personal appeal.

▲
The most controversial theologian of his era, JAMES PIKE *broke with formal religion in 1966, resigning as Episcopal Bishop of California amid accusations of heresy. He turned to spiritualism, trying to reach his dead son, and described his efforts in a book, "The Other Side." In 1969, while attempting to retrace the footsteps of "historical Jesus," he became lost in the Judean desert. His body was found seven days after his disappearance—in a kneeling position at the bottom of a precipice.*

▲
British hairdresser VIDAL SASSOON, *seen here atop some examples of his art, created a variety of distinctive hair styles, including his so-called "geometric cut" (above), "one-eyed girl," square curls and The Greek Goddess, that brought him fame—and rich clients—on both sides of the Atlantic. In 1967, when the script for the movie "Rosemary's Baby" called for actress Mia Farrow to have her hair cut by Sassoon, he was flown from London to Hollywood to do the job for $5,000—a hundred times his usual fee. On another occasion, the super-mod Sassoon refused to set an old-fashioned finger wave. "It's decadent," he explained.*

▲
"I would marry her without a stitch to her back," vowed former chauffeur ANDREI PORUMBEANU, *35, before eloping to North Carolina in 1960 with* GAMBLE BENEDICT, *19-year-old heiress to a $50 million fortune. But four years and two children later, the storybook romance was over. "Gambie" gained an annulment and soon married a policeman.*

▲
The wedding of JACQUELINE KENNEDY *and Greek shipping tycoon* ARISTOTLE ONASSIS *in 1968 linked one of the world's most glamorous women with one of the world's wealthiest men. He gave her jewelry worth five million dollars during their first year of marriage, prompting Jackie to confide: "Ari promised that, if I'm good, next year he'll give me the moon."*

An eloquent spokesman for the political right, acid-tongued author-columnist WILLIAM BUCKLEY *ran a tongue-in-cheek campaign as the Conservative Party's candidate for mayor of New York City in 1965. Admittedly out to swing votes away from liberal Republican John Lindsay, the self-consciously erudite Buckley offered such dazzlingly phrased proposals as an enlarged police force "enjoined to lust after the apprehension of criminals." Asked what he would do if elected, he quipped: "I'd demand a recount." To Buckley's dismay, his surprisingly large total of 340,000 votes — drawn mostly from conservative Democrats — assured Lindsay's election. Fellow conservative Barry Goldwater noted: "As a political kingmaker, you're a wrong-way Corrigan."*

▲

Boyish JULIAN BOND, *a civil rights militant who was once denied his seat in the Georgia legislature (it was subsequently restored to him by court decision) because of his anti-war views, was nominated for the Vice*

Presidency at the 1968 Democratic National Convention, the first Negro to be accorded that honor. But after polling 48½ votes, Bond withdrew from the race; at 28, he noted, he was seven years too young for the job.

The P. T. Barnum of the decade's New Left was University of California dropout JERRY RUBIN. *In 1968, he and fellow militant Abbie Hoffman gathered the "crazies on the left" into the Youth International Party — better known as Yippies — and held a mock convention in Chicago. There, in a slam at the cops and Democratic nominee Hubert Humphrey, they nominated a 200-pound pig named Pigasus for the Presidency. "The secret to the Yippie myth is that it's nonsense," explained Rubin, which accounted for the party's slogan, "Rise up and abandon the creeping meatball!", and its "most crucial" political issue: pay toilets.*

▶

173

The party of the decade was a masked ball thrown by elfin author TRUMAN CAPOTE *at the Plaza Hotel in New York City. Among the 500 "closest friends" invited by the host were Princess Peggy d'Arenberg (right, with Capote), artist Andy Warhol, actress Lauren Bacall, industrialist Henry Ford, poet Marianne Moore and novelist Norman Mailer. Also present were some of the gentry of Garden City, Kansas, locale of the quadruple murder in Capote's book "In Cold Blood," an elegant piece of police reporting that earned him two million dollars—or $14.80 each word.*

Former Brooklyn nursery-school teacher SHIRLEY CHISHOLM, *Democrat, beat Republican James Farmer, ex-head of* CORE, *by a huge 35,239 to 13,615 in 1968, becoming the first Negro Congresswoman. "My rise has been meteoric," said Mrs. Chisholm. "I know I am a symbol."*

Between the New Hampshire primary in March 1968 and the Democratic Convention in July, Senator EUGENE MC CARTHY *ran one of the most curious Presidential campaigns in history. Challenging current policies, especially the endless war in Vietnam, McCarthy attracted a devoted following, particularly among the disaffected young. But the closer he came to winning the nomination, the less he seemed to want it, and even before the Chicago countdown he had conceded defeat. Why had he entered the ring? Nobody seemed to know.*

◄ *"You are a gas," wired Beatle George Harrison to* TINY TIM, *quirkiest pop singer of the decade. Plinking his ukulele and squeaking out oldies like "Tiptoe through the Tulips" in a shrill falsetto, Herbert Buckingham Khaury gained fame on TV's top comedy show, "Laugh-In"—especially for a Victor Herbert duet with Carol Channing in which he sang Jeanette MacDonald to Carol's Nelson Eddy.*

▲ *Deadpan humor, a perfect sense of timing and the ability to mix urbanity with boyish charm lofted* JOHNNY CARSON *to the top of the late-night TV talk shows. As host of NBC's top-rated "Tonight," Carson regularly drew 35 per cent of all the nightly viewers and after a celebrated salary walkout in 1967, was reputedly earning $25,000 a week.*

In race-troubled Cleveland, Democrat CARL STOKES, *great-grandson of a slave, entered the race for mayor in 1967 opposing Republican Seth Taft, grandson of a U.S. President. Stokes won by a slim margin of 1,644 votes to become the first Negro mayor of a major U.S. city.*
▼

◄ *Trading on her real-life experiences as a housewife ("I never use any words that you can't hear in a supermarket") rubber-faced comedienne* PHYLLIS DILLER *put on a ratatat nightclub routine that won her roles as comedian Bob Hope's leading lady in three movies and an invitation to be the sixth Dolly in the Broadway musical "Hello Dolly."*

In 1965 author NORMAN MAILER published his first novel in 10 years, "An American Dream." The critics roasted it. In 1967, when he took part in an antiwar march on the Pentagon, one reporter described him as "pathetic" and "booze-soaked." A few months later, Mailer published his account of that march, "The Armies of the Night," and in 1969 it won both the National Book Award and the Pulitzer Prize. On the crest of this wave, Mailer teamed with fellow writer Jimmy Breslin to wage a bombastic campaign for mayor of New York. He lost, naturally, but gained a world of publicity. And to defray the $40,000 in political expenses, there was one million dollars in advance royalties for his newest book, a report on the first moon shot, "A Fire on the Moon."

▲
Scottish actor SEAN CONNERY *played two-fisted, supersexy secret agent James Bond in five movies based on British author Ian Fleming's best-selling spy novels. His swashbuckling portrayal earned him a salary that rose from $30,000 for the first Bond epic, 1963's "Dr. No," to $750,000 a picture by 1966. In 1965 he was the country's top box-office star. But he was also tired of playing Bond, and in 1967 he quit the role; three years later he won high praise as a miner in the grim film "The Molly Maguires."*

▲
In 1968 folk singer PETE SEEGER, *taping a guest shot for the irreverent Smothers Brothers show, sang an antiwar song. Network censors cut it from the program—but after a storm of protest, they let him sing it six months later on the same show.*

▲
Loser-of-the-decade in publishing was RALPH GINZBURG. *When he put out a high-class ($25 a subscription) sex magazine called "Eros" in 1962, the Post Office labeled it obscene and Ginzburg got a five-year jail term. "Eros" folded. While appealing his sentence, Ginzburg began an exposé-type bimonthly, "Fact," in 1964. But "Fact" printed some dubious facts about 1964 Presidential candidate Barry Goldwater, who sued for libel and won $75,000. "Fact" folded. In 1967 Ginzburg started yet another magazine, "Avant-Garde." Its forte was erotica; but by that time movies, plays and books had become so wildly sexy that even Ginzburg said that next to an opus like "Portnoy's Complaint," "Avant-Garde" was sadly (and unprofitably) in the ruck.*

In 1964 commercial artist PETER MAX, then 25, had a vision: "I saw a huge monumental wave of youth—the youth revolution coming." He promptly set out to create an art for the new age: bright-colored designs that mixed images from nature (stars, flowers) with abstract patterns (circles, checkerboards). Vibrating on posters, decals, china, scarves, ads, etc., Max's psychedelic art form earned him a groovy yearly income of two million dollars by 1969.

Defector of the decade was Soviet dictator Joseph Stalin's daughter, SVETLANA ALLILUYEVA, who was given political asylum in the U.S. in April 1967. Six months later she published her memoirs of life in the Kremlin, "Twenty Letters to a Friend." Though reviewers found little that was new in it and thought its portrait of Stalin rather gentle, it earned her a tidy three million dollars. In her second book, "Only One Year" (September 1969), Svetlana took a harder line

with her father, calling him "a moral and spiritual monster." She also expressed boundless enthusiasm for "rosy-cheeked, blue-eyed" America, which she embraced first by buying a $60,000 house in Princeton, New Jersey. Then, in April 1970, three years after she had first debarked in New York with a bright "Hello there, everyone" for the airport crowd, she took the final step toward Americanization by marrying an Arizona architect, William Peters.

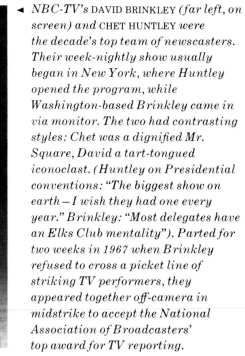

NBC-TV's DAVID BRINKLEY (far left, on screen) and CHET HUNTLEY were the decade's top team of newscasters. Their week-nightly show usually began in New York, where Huntley opened the program, while Washington-based Brinkley came in via monitor. The two had contrasting styles: Chet was a dignified Mr. Square, David a tart-tongued iconoclast. (Huntley on Presidential conventions: "The biggest show on earth—I wish they had one every year." Brinkley: "Most delegates have an Elks Club mentality"). Parted for two weeks in 1967 when Brinkley refused to cross a picket line of striking TV performers, they appeared together off-camera in midstrike to accept the National Association of Broadcasters' top award for TV reporting.

177

In a time of increasing sexual freedom on campuses, Vassar President SARAH GIBSON BLANDING made it plain that hanky-panky was not for her. Calling a compulsory assembly one day in 1962, she told her 1,450 girls to stay chaste or leave the campus. Nobody left, but everyone started to shout. "If Vassar is to become the Poughkeepsie Victorian Seminary for Young Virgins," shrilled one girl, it "had better be made explicit in the admissions catalogue." Newspapers had a field day; Miss Blanding held fast. "Some people assume I'm against young romance. There's not a bit of truth in it. I'm always pleased as punch to meet the girls' beaux," she said, in a tone that clearly meant the place for a beau was still the drawing room.

▼

Chicago's Mayor RICHARD DALEY, already a legend of sorts in his hometown, won national fame during the Democratic Convention of 1968 when his police force beat up youthful demonstrators in full view of the TV audience. "Gentlemen, get the thing straight once and for all," he later told newsmen in defending the cops, "the policeman isn't there to create disorder, the policeman is there to preserve disorder." This kind of heroic malapropism had long been Daley's stock in trade. "I resent the insinuendos," he had said in 1965, when his administration was charged with corruption; and in looking forward to bigger and better things for the Windy City: "Together we must rise to ever higher and higher platitudes."

She was a rarity in the '60s, someone who spanned the generation gap, appealing to hip kids and senior citizens alike. Her name, BARBRA STREISAND; her forte, singing—via four media: Broadway, recordings, TV and movies. She had never had a vocal lesson in her life; she didn't need one. "To me a song is a role to be acted out," she said, and that was exactly what she did, now belting, now wistful, now bluesy—a range that had something for everyone.

▶

▶

◀ THE SMOTHERS BROTHERS, Tom and Dick, had TV's top-rated Sunday night show—until they lost their $4.5 million contract in a censorship tiff with CBS. "Painters can reflect their society," said Tom. "And writers can. Why can't TV comedians?" The network declined to answer the question, but the position of Smothers fans was clear enough: they picketed the CBS Building in New York.

French chef JULIA CHILD, *a six-foot two-inch bundle of good sense and bons mots, drew three million viewers weekly on educational TV stations while she tossed up haute cuisine —and never lost her poise when facing small catastrophes. "Remember," she said, "you're all alone in the kitchen and no one can see you"—at which point she retrieved a dropped potato pancake and tossed it into the frying pan. And when the prop men forgot and left the butter in the refrigerator she ad-libbed: "I'm rather glad this happened because I can tell you what to do if you've left YOUR butter in the refrigerator and you find it is much too hard to work with." Whereupon she put it over a low flame and finished the show on time.*

◄ *The beaming lady pointing in triumph to the bestseller list is* JACQUELINE SUSANN, *mistress of the raunchy sex novel that came close to dominating American fiction during the '60s. Author Susann earned more than one million dollars on "Valley of the Dolls," her first novel, and doubled that on her second, "The Love Machine." The books were panned by the critics, but Jackie couldn't care less. "There's no room for deathless prose in the novel," she said.*

▲

"A year ago I was talking about the war in Vietnam," said DR. BENJAMIN SPOCK *in 1969; "in spring I was talking about the stifling of dissent. The focus shifts." Spock's focus certainly did. The 1946 author of the world's best-selling baby book, Spock had written for mamas; he was now counseling their children to evade the draft.*

As the civil rights movement gathered force, the writings of novelist JAMES BALDWIN ("Go Tell It on the Mountain," "Another Country") took an angry turn from character analysis to militancy. His blistering 1963 essay, "The Fire Next Time," and a 1964 play, "Blues for Mr. Charlie," bitterly telling every white man how much every black man hated him, catapulted Baldwin into the front lines of the race struggle. ▼

In 1963 BETTY FRIEDAN, a suburban housewife and mother of three, wrote "The Feminine Mystique," a book angrily blasting American women's domestic bondage. The book helped to trigger a powerful new emancipation movement called Women's Liberation, which manifested itself in everything from public burning of brassieres to well-financed Washington lobbies asking for strict enforcement of the fair-employment laws.

© 1969 by United Feature Syndicate, Inc.

▲

SNOOPY was the hero of Charles Schultz's comic strip "Peanuts," avidly read by 90 million. The strip became a $20 million industry, whose artifacts included books, records, sweat shirts, pillows and TV specials.

◄ "Sex and the Single Girl," the first book by advertising copywriter HELEN GURLEY BROWN, became an overnight bestseller in 28 countries and 17 languages. Observing these phenomenal sales, "Cosmopolitan," a woman's magazine with lagging revenues, hired Mrs. Brown as editor to try to change the magazine's fortunes. She promptly turned "Cosmo" into a bible for single girls whose assumed goal was to have a glorious love life. Mrs. Brown's columns advised girls to wear false eyelashes, keep at least one rich beau on hand for fancy restaurants and flirt hard at the office—with someone else's boss. In three years "Cosmopolitan's" ad revenues more than doubled.

When Harlem's flamboyant Congressman, ADAM CLAYTON POWELL, refused to pay a $164,000 court judgment—and his fellow Congressmen decided he had also misused $40,000 in funds—he was denied his seat in the House of Representatives. Powell remained suspended for two years, most of which he spent basking on Bimini Island in the Atlantic. The 1969 Congress restored his seat to him.
▼

"Extremism in the defense of liberty is no vice . . . moderation in the pursuit of justice is no virtue." With these radical words, Arizona's arch-conservative, Senator BARRY GOLDWATER, accepted the nomination as the Republican candidate for President in 1964. Despite such fervor, and his "Go with Goldwater" slogan (note glasses), he went on to sustain one of the worst defeats in Presidential campaign history.
▼

Nixon's Vice President, SPIRO T. AGNEW, turned his job into a pulpit for attacks on those he saw as Administration foes. He exhorted against network TV newscasters ("a small and unelected elite") and the Vietnam Moratorium, whose leaders he labeled "an effete corps of impudent snobs." Antiwar protestors turned Agnew's rhetoric back at him by sporting buttons reading "Effete Snobs for Peace."
▼

In 1962 EDWARD ALBEE brought out his first full-length play, a witches' brew of domestic love/hate called "Who's Afraid of Virginia Woolf?". Probing the relationship between a middle-aged professor and his wife, Albee's dialogue shocked Broadway audiences for 664 performances with its destructive interpretation of an American marriage:
GEORGE: You can sit there in that chair of yours, you can sit there with the gin running out of your mouth, and you can humiliate me, you can tear me apart . . . all night . . . and that's perfectly all right . . . that's O.K.
MARTHA: You can stand it!
GEORGE: I cannot stand it!
MARTHA: You can stand it!! You married me for it!!
Said Albee about this assault on the facades of social existence: "Some people spend all their time being political activists. Others teach. Others go out to assassinate people. I write plays."

Columnist SUZY KNICKERBOCKER *amused readers in 60 newspapers with saucy gossip about the decade's jet-setters. Asked, "Do you take all this society stuff seriously?" she replied, "Good heavens, does anyone?"*

Bragging that he was "the greatest" and coining homemade verse ("They all must fall/in the round I call"), prizefighter CASSIUS CLAY *astounded the boxing world by proving he was right. In 1964 he became world heavyweight champion by beating Sonny Liston. Two days after the title bout he suddenly announced his conversion to the Black Muslim faith, and three years later, under the Muslim name of Muhammad Ali, he defiantly refused induction into the Army on grounds of conscience. Stripped of his title by most boxing commissions, Ali waited out the disposition of his draft appeal by taking on such odd jobs as playing the lead in the Broadway musical "Buck White."*

Offered her first film role, "Mary Poppins" (above), Broadway star JULIE ANDREWS *hesitated. "Work for Walt Disney? The cartoon person?" she asked a friend. But work for him she did—and went on to become Hollywood's third-ranking money maker, earning one million dollars and more per picture.*

ANDY WARHOL, *pioneer of pop art, asked by a dealer what was the most important thing in his life, replied "Money." Painter Warhol amassed great sums of it by creating such high camp masterpieces as giant-size Brillo boxes ($3,000) and outsize paintings of Campbell's soup cans ($45,000). Then he made still more by*

filming interminable, plotless movies, such as "The Chelsea Girls" ($500,000 gross receipts), in which girls, boys and various in-between types somehow kept forgetting to put on any clothes. To art critics Andy's creations were "mordant affirmations and biting parodies"; to Andy they were "just marvelous."

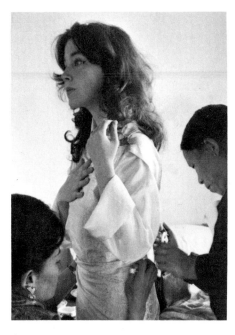

Sarah Lawrence graduate HOPE COOKE was the only American of the decade to acquire a country all her own: in 1963 she married Prince Palden Thondup Namgyal of the tiny Himalayan kingdom of Sikkim.

▲

Scandal rocked Washington in 1962, when West Texas fertilizer magnate BILLIE SOL ESTES, a nonsmoking, nondrinking, ex-farmboy, was caught selling $24 million in mortgage papers on nonexistent storage tanks — all the while lavishing gifts on government men. Said Senator John McClellan, Billie's adventures were "the darnedest mess I've ever seen."

RICHARD NIXON, beaten by John Kennedy in the 1960 Presidential election and then beaten again by incumbent Pat Brown in a race for governor of California, bid "farewell to politics" in 1962. But in 1968 he staged an awesome comeback, beating Democrat Hubert Humphrey for the Presidency with the aid of a multi-million dollar TV campaign.

◄ Crusading biologist RACHEL CARSON threw the $330 million pesticide industry for a hefty loss with the 1962 publication of "Silent Spring," in which she argued with scientific savvy and poetic grace that certain pesticides would "still the song of birds and the leaping of fish in the streams." Indeed she was certain that pesticides threatened man himself. The industry called her emotional and ignorant. But a Presidential committee that studied pesticides confirmed many of Miss Carson's most alarming theses; and by decade's end, at least five state legislatures had either banned or limited the use of DDT, and production was down 20 per cent.

▼

Middle America

Half a Nation

It's really too bad we—the Middle Americans, or whatever you want to call us—don't have an articulate spokesman. The average American still holds to honesty, decency, integrity, enterprise and so on but maybe we've been so busy doing our own thing that we've failed to be vigilant in guarding these virtues.

OPIE SHELTON, ATLANTA CHAMBER OF COMMERCE

Some 40 miles west of Kansas City, Kansas, Route 70 heads into Lawrence, a residential and industrial center of 49,000. On the outskirts, a turn-off called 8th Street leads past a few shacky beer joints to a stark building with the look of an abandoned warehouse. Inside is the office of paper-company executive Stephen Hill—a good-looking young man of 33 with strong feelings about his America, far removed from the world of hippies, drugs and riots. "I have a deep sense that this kind of life as we know it here is passing," said Hill to a Chicago reporter, "the kind of life in which people have back lawns and front lawns, the kind of life in which it takes me five minutes to get to the office and five minutes after I get home to be out in the country to go hunting. This sort of life has a lot to do with my values."

It had a lot to do with the values of a great many other Americans, too—at least 100 million of them. Though some lived in places like Peacham, Vermont *(right)*, they were mainly represented in the heartland *(following pages)*, where life had not changed much since these people had been growing up. To customers in these towns, Sears, Roebuck was still selling wood-stoked stoves and manually operated ice cream freezers and J.C. Penney was selling 100,000 elastic-bound bloomers a year.

For much of the decade, these stable, tradition-loving people felt substantially unrepresented. Then, in 1968 they found their voice in Presidential nominee Richard M. Nixon, who called on these "forgotten Americans" to help him guide the country back to the values they cherished.

While other Americans were vigorously criticizing some of those values, Middle America began to stand up and demand to be counted. Patriotic flag decals appeared on cars, home and store windows and even baby carriages. *Reader's Digest* distributed 68,441,-368 such paste-ons and Tiffany's in New York offered a 14-carat lapel flag "for those who are still as proud of the American flag as we are." And as the U.S. moved into the '70s, a poll by *Life* magazine of a cross section of Americans provided this revelation: 95 per cent most wanted "green grass and trees around me," while 82 per cent considered "to be at peace with yourself and have honest relations with others" to be the two most important goals in life.

A retired dairyman leaves one of his favorite hangouts, the icicle-hung general store in Peacham, Vermont, a village of 500.

Pulling up his tractor to a homemade gas tank, a farmer in Putnam County, Indiana, and his tiny helper prepare to refuel.

A Kentucky coal miner endures his baptism in the snow-mottled water of a winter stream.

Snuggled around a corner table, three ladies of Abilene, Kansas, enjoy a long coffee klatsch at Harry Simmers' drugstore.

In town for a few hours, cronies in Batesville, Arkansas, camp on a rail on Main Street while their wives are off shopping.

Attentive civic leaders hear out a candidate running for state senate at a 7:30 a.m. breakfast meeting in Greencastle, Indiana.

Members of Greencastle's First Christian Church attend a barbecue.

Peering at the music, a piano teacher in Manchester, Iowa, encourages a nine-year-old as he performs Brahms' "Lullaby."

From cars, curbside deck chairs, lawns and roofs, spectators watch a Memorial Day parade in Ticonderoga, New York.

Doves and Hawks

Hands raised in the peace sign, Manhattan, 1969.

The Troubled Crusade

That's what really bothers me about this war. Sometimes I feel like one of the bad guys. I mean in World War II it was more clear-cut. You know, the Nazis on one side and us on the other.

MARINE IN VIETNAM, 1965

John F. Kennedy used to tell a story about the outbreak of World War I: after the diplomatic negotiations in the long summer of 1914 terminated in war, the German Chancellor, Bethmann-Hollweg, was approached by his predecessor, Prince Von Bülow. "How did it all begin?" Von Bülow asked. The Chancellor answered slowly: "Ach, if one could only say."

So it was with Americans throughout the 1960s; as they bickered over a war in which victory seemed unattainable and defeat unacceptable, no one could say how it had happened. Yet as they looked back at decade's end, the steps appeared so clear.

President Kennedy had inherited from the Truman and Eisenhower regimes a commitment to prevent a Communist takeover in South Vietnam, a small, weak Southeast Asian country formed in 1954 from a coastal strip of the former French colony of Indochina. To keep this tiny ally from going down the Red drain, Kennedy increased the amount of aid to the South Vietnamese government. Where President Truman had sent 35 military advisers and Ike had sent some 500 more, Kennedy sent 16,000. And where the first advisers did little but train South

Vietnamese troops, by 1962 the south's military position had so deteriorated that J.F.K. authorized U.S. helicopters to fire at the enemy; and a year later he permitted them to fly strafing missions. Some of the first American combat casualties were Green Berets, elite troops especially trained in guerrilla warfare and sent to Asia by Kennedy.

No roars of protest went up from the public; no eyebrows rose in Congress; no editorialists thundered as the United States suffered its casualties and increased its aid in matériel and in men. For the American presence in Vietnam was completely within the context of President Truman's broad policy, established in 1947, of stopping cold any further Communist advances anywhere in the world. This doctrine of containment had worked from Azerbaijan to Greece to Trieste to Korea to Berlin. To doubt it seemed not only unpatriotic but unreasonable.

The majority feeling about Vietnam then was one of approval; Americans were proud of what they were doing for the "free peoples of Vietnam" and repeated President Eisenhower's domino theory about the non-Communist states of Southeast Asia ("You

Green Berets fall in at their home base, looking, as a current ballad about them put it, like "men who mean just what they say."

have a row of dominoes. You knock over the first one and the last one will go over very quickly"). "The Ballad of the Green Berets," written later by a Special Forces sergeant in South Vietnam, unabashedly told of the nation's pride in doing its duty:

> *Put silver wings on my son's chest,*
> *Make him one of America's best.*
> *He'll be a man they'll test one day—*
> *Have him win the green beret.*

Kennedy's 1963 State of the Union message contained this confident assessment: "The spear point of aggression has been blunted in South Vietnam." The fact is, his conclusion was not only premature but ironic. On April 6, 1954, after a trip to Vietnam, young Senator John F. Kennedy of Massachusetts had scathingly criticized "predictions of confidence which have lulled the American people." Yet seven years later, having abandoned the role of Senate critic for that of President, Kennedy succumbed to the momentum of the established policy and kept on escalating the U.S. commitment.

Upon Kennedy's death, Vietnam beckoned another wise man away from his earlier convictions. As far back as 1954, Senate Minority Leader Lyndon Johnson bitterly and successfully had opposed the Dulles-Eisenhower plan for a U.S. carrier strike at the North Vietnamese Reds. In 1961 Vice President Lyndon Johnson, fresh from a trip to Vietnam, reported to his chief that "American combat troop involvement is not only not required, it is not desirable." However, President Lyndon Johnson thought differently—just as President Kennedy had.

By 1964 governments had come and gone so fast in the southern capital of Saigon that President Johnson felt compelled to lead the U.S. in deeper, hoping to stabilize the situation. On August 4, 1964, reacting vigorously to confused Navy reports that North Vietnamese torpedo craft had attacked two U.S. destroyers in the Gulf of Tonkin, L.B.J. sent

U.S. planes to bomb North Vietnam. The country gave him broad support. According to a Lou Harris poll, 85 per cent of the nation approved the bombing.

The Senate also supported the aggressive policy. Immediately after Tonkin the Administration asked Congressional approval of a White House-written resolution authorizing the President to take "all necessary steps including the use of armed force" to defend the free states in Southeast Asia. Scholarly Senator William J. Fulbright, chairman of the Foreign Relations Committee, personally floor-managed the resolution in the Senate, guiding it to approval after only nine hours of debate—less time than the Senate usually took to amend a fisheries' bill. Liberals such as Eugene McCarthy, Albert Gore, George McGovern and Birch Bayh approved. The press favored the move. *The Washington Post:* "President Johnson has earned the gratitude of the free world." *The New York Times:* "The nation's united confidence in the Chief Executive is vital." Over the next year, the nation stayed behind L.B.J. as he escalated from a policy of retaliation to one of continuous bombing.

And now America was in it for fair. What had begun a decade before as a routine commitment to containment was on its way to becoming the third most costly foreign war in U.S. history. By 1966 L.B.J. had raised U.S. armed forces in Vietnam twenty-fold over the previous year to 375,000. U.S. units were often taking higher casualties than the South Vietnamese; the weekly bomb tonnage dropped on North Vietnam exceeded the bombs dropped on Germany during the height of World War II; and the war was costing the U.S. $25 billion a year.

It had also become Lyndon Johnson's personal war. He himself picked the bombing targets; and almost every morning at 3 o'clock, according to a later account by his brother Sam, "he would crawl out of bed, wearily slip on his robe and slippers, then go down to the Situation Room in the basement of the

A South Vietnamese guard threatens a Viet Cong captive.

White House to get the latest reports coming in from Saigon." Though privately he might call Vietnam "a mess," less privately he sneered at war critics as "Nervous Nellies." As the year passed, these Presidential snarls took on an increasingly defensive tone; and no wonder. For a tide of skepticism was rising, not strong at first, but strong enough to earn its expressers the factional nickname of Doves—as opposed to the Hawks, or warbackers.

Foremost among the Doves' concerns was a growing uneasiness about what was going on inside Vietnam. Word was filtering back of what lay beneath the military talk of body counts and kill ratios. TV cameras showed U.S. Marines casually setting Vietnamese villages on fire with cigarette lighters (some units called themselves Zippo squads). There were photos of children scarred by napalm, of prisoners threatened by torture, reports on the damage done to humans and their crops by a U.S. campaign to defoliate enemy-occupied areas with chemicals. The image of South Vietnam as a brave little democracy was also getting frayed. Now Americans were told that 50 per cent of U.S. aid went directly into the black market, that the Vietnam desertion rate was more than 15 per cent, that in any event well-to-do Vietnamese youngsters could quite easily buy their way out of the draft.

Americans, used to fighting wars they considered just, wars that began with a date, a cause ("Remember the Maine!"), grew increasingly confused and disheartened; they didn't know when they had started fighting or why. They only knew that more and more Americans were being drafted and being killed; and they were less and less convinced it was for a good reason. The misgivings were contagious, intensified by each new casualty list, each new atrocity report. And the more deeply the U.S. became involved, the more the misgivings grew until Administration adviser Cyrus Vance warned that they were "threatening to tear the United States apart."

The Antiwar Protest

In July 1968, six years after he joined his first peace march, Dr. Benjamin Spock was sentenced to two years in jail (later reversed) for conspiring to counsel draft evaders. His increased involvement in the antiwar movement reflected the escalation in the movement itself. As the decade started, it scarcely existed. By October 1967, 35,000 war critics were participating in a march on Washington. In November 1969, more than 250,000 protesters staged the biggest demonstration in the capital's history.

The protest, like the tragedy of the war itself, took many forms *(following pages)*. While men died on the battlefield, at home there were antiwar musical shows, pacifist folk songs, sit-ins for peace. In November 1965 two young protesters burned themselves to death. Congress was disrupted in September 1967 when five demonstrators rained a shower of antiwar leaflets on the Senate floor. In Washington Catholic priests ransacked the offices of a napalm-producing chemical company in March 1969. On Moratorium Day, October 15, 1969, a handful of GIs in Vietnam went out on patrol wearing black armbands—the M-Day symbol of dissent. The same year New York City's Mayor John Lindsay, campaigning for reelection, threw his support behind the war protests—and won.

By the decade's end, protest seemed to be gaining favor: a nationwide poll after the October Moratorium showed only 45 per cent of Americans were "not in sympathy" with antiwar demonstrations.

We demand that no more American youth be sent to fight in a war that is helping neither them nor the Vietnamese people. We have learned lessons from Nazi Germany, and will not go along with the aggressive war-making policies of any government, even if it happens to be our own.

FIFTH AVENUE VIETNAM PEACE PARADE COMMITTEE

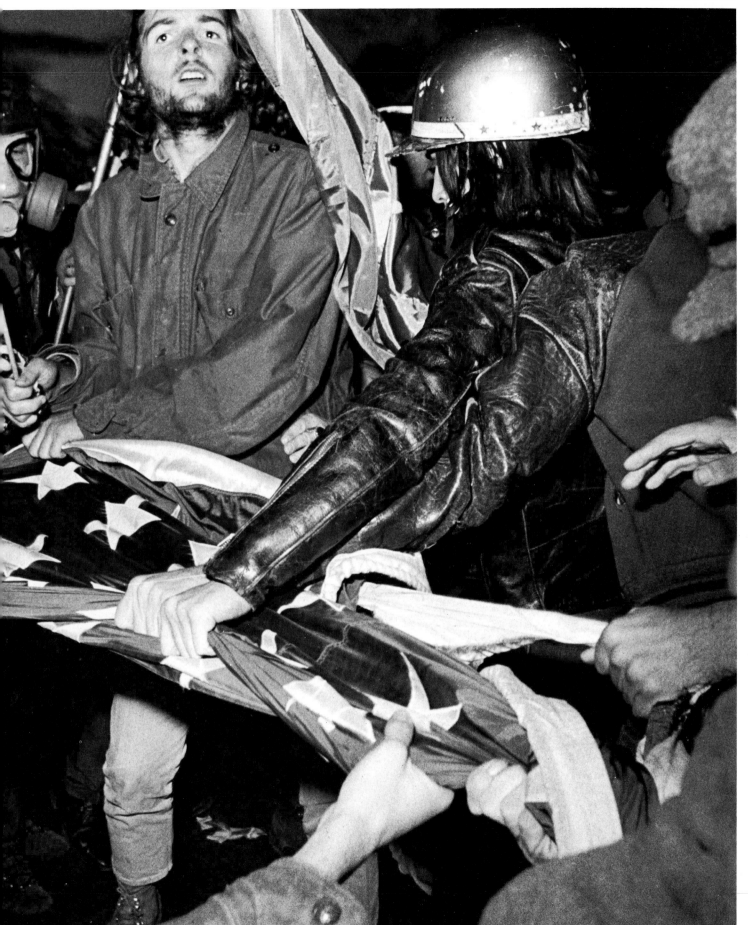

Youths at a Washington, D.C., rally rip the Stars from the Stripes to protest what some called the "immoral" Vietnam war.

Viet Cong guerrillas lie dead following a battle in the Mekong River Delta.

How many dead men will it take
To build a dike that will not break,
How many children must we kill
Before we make the waves stand still?
Though miracles come high today,
We have the wherewithal to pay,
It takes them off the streets you know
To places they would never go alone....
How many men to conquer Mars,
How many dead to reach the stars?

"SAIGON BRIDE" BY NINA DUSHECK AND JOAN BAEZ

Folk singer Joan Baez, who served a jail term for her part in antiwar demonstrations, popularized the songs of protest.

In the surrealistic musical "Promenade," two wounded GIs trying to figure out how they got into the war in the first place are interrupted by civilians bent on pleasure as usual.

FIRST SOLDIER: *Did you volunteer?*

SECOND SOLDIER: *For what?*

FIRST SOLDIER: *To get the bombs dropped on you.*

SECOND SOLDIER: *No, I didn't. . . . I was going home from work when someone said: "Hey, soldier!" and I made the mistake to look.*

FIRST SOLDIER: *You volunteered then.*

SECOND SOLDIER: *Why?*

FIRST SOLDIER: *Because you looked.*

SECOND SOLDIER: *Gosh, I shouldn't have looked.*

FIRST SOLDIER: *Well, they get you anyway. . . .*

CIVILIANS *(singing and dancing around them):* *It's springtime and hepaticas are blooming.*

PROMENADE, ACT II, SCENE I

Homefront revelers in "Promenade" turn two wounded GIs into human Maypoles, unwinding their bandages for ribbons.

The suffering of real-life soldiers such as these Americans on a Vietnam hill inspired the protest theater's bitter message.

The Art of Draft Dodging

In 1966 monthly draft calls shot up almost tenfold over 1965's figures of 5,000 per month. To fill the quotas, blanket student deferments were abolished and many college boys were reclassified. Campuses erupted in protest: University of Chicago students seized and held the administration building for three days; 500 professors from 50 institutions formed an ad hoc committee to oppose the new system.

Open, active draft resistance took on a major role in youth's dissent against the Establishment. Buttons, ballads, bumper stickers and posters socked the message to the country. A popular song, Arlo Guthrie's "Alice's Restaurant," included a wildly satirical account of Guthrie's efforts to hornswaggle a draftboard psychiatrist into giving a deferment. Another technique was suggested in a pamphlet handed out by a protest group on college campuses: "Arrive high. If you want to go about the addiction scene in a really big way, use a common pin on your arm for a few weeks in advance." By 1968 an estimated 10,000 eligible Americans had taken the drastic step of emigrating to Canada, where organizations like Toronto's Students Union for Peace Action helped newcomers adjust to what might be permanent exile.

And I walked in, I sat down, they gave me a piece of paper that said: Kid, see the psychiatrist, Room 604. I went up there, I said, "Shrink, I wanna kill. I wanna kill! I wanna see blood and gore and guts and veins in my teeth! Eat dead, burnt bodies! I mean: Kill, kill!" And I started jumpin' up and down, yellin', "KILL! KILL!" and he started jumpin' up and down with me, and we was both jumpin' up and down, yellin', "KILL, KILL," and the sergeant came over, pinned a medal on me.

"ALICE'S RESTAURANT" BY ARLO GUTHRIE

A photo of alleged antidraft émigrés became a popular poster.

A lapel button (top) announces an antidraft week, and a sticker and a poster suggest pleasant alternatives to soldiering.

A flower child spikes the guns of military police guarding the Pentagon during a peace protest by 35,000 people in 1967.

Candles light up the night on October 15, 1969, as a million Americans—including these in Miami—call for a war Moratorium.

moratorium

Marchers in Washington improvise candleholders.

Anti-Protest Protest

By no means all Americans—even young Americans—opposed the war. As protests against the Vietnam involvement increased, a counterwave of prowar feeling arose from youth groups such as the Young Americans for Freedom, the established military boosters like the American Legion and Veterans of Foreign Wars, and some public figures such as California Governor Ronald Reagan. Though President Nixon described these traditionalists as the silent majority, they were in fact increasingly vocal. In speeches they urged military victory or gradual withdrawal and accused dissenters of encouraging the enemy. Their biggest demonstration, on Veterans' Day 1969 during a National Unity Week, drew crowds across the country (the largest, in Birmingham, numbered over 100,000) in support of U.S. war policy.

Calling the silent majority. Fed up with defeatist demands? Don't gripe. Speak out!
VETERANS' DAY HANDBILL, WASHINGTON, D.C.

If we ever let the Communists win this war, we are in great danger of fighting for the rest of our lives and losing a million kids.
BOB HOPE, CO-CHAIRMAN, NATIONAL UNITY WEEK

I suppose the protesters have a right to their point of view, but I just think they're wrong. There just isn't any way of winning this war militarily. That's why President Nixon is trying to get us out with some degree of honor. But the only way he can do that is if we present a united front.
CALIFORNIA HOUSEWIFE AT VETERANS' DAY PARADE

We won't creep around in the dark with candles like these traitors do. We'll march at high noon and let free people fall right in and march behind us.
POLICE CHIEF DALLAS BIAS, CHARLESTON, WEST VIRGINIA

Protesting an earlier peace march by 30 persons, some young Floridians head for a "We Love America" rally that drew 300.

Americans — prowar and antiwar — united in deploring the conflict's tragic toll, which by 1970 had caused the deaths of 300,000 South Vietnamese civilians. These excerpts are from letters written by U.S. personnel in Vietnam.

They've been hit by napalm bombs, hand grenades, mortars (not all by V.C. either; many are hit by mistake by friendly forces) . . . wrinkled old men and women who appear to have aged with the earth itself; younger people, old before their time . . . children and tiny babies who lose limbs or become otherwise scarred before their lives have really begun.
U.S. CIVILIAN NURSE, APRIL 1966

Our battalion managed to retake the town by daybreak. When we moved in only one person was left alive in the place: a small boy who was badly wounded.
ADVISORY TEAM MEMBER, APRIL 1966

Under Viet Cong fire, a medic dashes for shelter to treat a little boy wounded by a strafing U.S. jet. The child later died.

A veteran of Senator Eugene McCarthy's anti-war crusade shows up in Washington for the inauguration of Richard Nixon.

The Long Road Back

By 1968 the opposition to the Vietnam war was pressing in from all sides. The campuses, long a focal point of dissent, were now feverish with sit-ins and strikes; in the first semester of the 1967-1968 academic year, there were 204 separate demonstrations, most of them associated with opposition to the war. Draft cards were burned and induction centers picketed to chants of "Hey, hey, LBJ/How many kids did you kill today?" "Hell no, we won't go," was another favorite slogan, and indeed 22 per cent of Harvard's seniors said in January 1968 they would rather go to jail or into exile than into the Army. Hesitantly at first, then more readily, their elders began to make themselves heard as well. In April 1967 Martin Luther King Jr., joined by 46 Harvard professors, announced "Vietnam Summer," an antiwar campaign. On January 5, 1968, Yale chaplain William Sloane Coffin Jr. was indicted for allegedly conspiring to counsel young men on how to avoid the draft. And on February 29, diplomat George Kennan made a major attack on the war policy.

Then, on the afternoon of Monday, January 29, 1968, as the Tet festival of the New Year dawned in South Vietnam, the Doves in America received terrible confirmation of all their worst doubts. The enemy, whom U.S. diplomats and field commanders had reported to be in a state of exhaustion, suddenly unleashed his greatest offensive of the war. In 72 shattering hours the Communist forces captured the large city of Hué and fought their way into the grounds of the supposedly impenetrable U.S. Embassy in Saigon, where they held out for six hours. Though the U.S. Army in Vietnam numbered a half million men, American soldiers took until February 20 to dislodge the enemy from the rest of Saigon and until February 24 to free Hué.

The Communist Tet offensive was carried out with a violence that shatteringly denied all the official descriptions of an exhausted enemy. Much of the American public had believed the U.S. was winning; now it knew otherwise. In an effort to revive confidence, General William Westmoreland, commander of the American forces in Vietnam, pointing out that 42,000 of the enemy had died, protested that Viet Cong plans "went afoul." But now his optimism was openly challenged in the highest places. Senator Robert Kennedy, who had earlier supported his brother's escalation in Vietnam, declared that Tet "shattered the mask of official illusion under which we concealed our true circumstances, even from ourselves." Senator Fulbright, who had floor-managed the 1964 Tonkin Gulf Resolution, giving President Johnson virtually unlimited war powers in Vietnam, protested that he had been duped: "I did a great disservice to the Senate. I regret it more than anything I have ever done in my life." In a post-Tet special broadcast, NBC concluded: "The initiative has passed to the enemy." Walter Cronkite, senior newsman at CBS, reported that the U.S. was mired in a "military stalemate" and threatened with "cosmic disaster."

Still striving for victory, General Westmoreland asked for another 206,000 men – a 40 per cent rise in a force level that had already crept up to 510,000. The Joint Chiefs of Staff approved. But now President Johnson showed private signs of doubt and sought advice from former President Truman's Secretary of State, Dean Acheson. Acheson said: "With all due respect, Mr. President, the Joint Chiefs of Staff don't know what they're talking about." That was shocking, the President said. Well, said Acheson, perhaps the President ought to be shocked.

Yet L.B.J. was still not ready to reverse the U.S. commitment. He called in Clark Clifford, a Hawk and a loyal Johnson man, to replace Defense Secretary Robert McNamara, who Johnson believed had gone soft on Vietnam. Clifford studied Westmoreland's request for reinforcements and, to L.B.J.'s surprise, advised against it. Johnson now concurred; and what was more, he recalled General Westmoreland.

The course of escalation had been stopped. But for

Lyndon Baines Johnson the politician, there were some indications that the move might have come too late. Primary elections aimed at selecting the 1968 Presidential candidates were at hand, the first in New Hampshire on March 12 and the next in Wisconsin, April 2. And Johnson suddenly discovered that his career was at stake. Thoroughly disaffected by the war, Minnesota Senator Eugene McCarthy, once close enough to L.B.J. to be considered for his 1964 running mate, had decided to challenge Johnson for the '68 Presidential nomination.

McCarthy's announcement seemed, at first, like a tilt by Don Quixote at the world's biggest windmill. McCarthy began the New Hampshire campaign with no visible political organization, no funds and not even a staff. But suddenly, in one of the most striking, spontaneous occurrences in the history of American politics, some 5,000 college boys and girls began pouring into New Hampshire to set up 15 McCarthy campaign centers. Shaven, shorn and neatened up to solicit conservative backing for their champion, the kids pinned McCarthy buttons on factory workers and pleaded with housewives to consider McCarthy's candidacy on a peace ticket. Given a chance at only 12 per cent of the vote by the Gallup Poll in January, then 18 per cent by a secret L.B.J. poll in February, and 25 to 28 per cent by another prediction in early March, McCarthy actually won a thundering 28,791 total votes to 29,021 for the President. This gave Johnson and his powerful professional machine a lead of only 230 ballots — and this in a conservative, nominally Hawkish state. The startling results made it no longer impossible that McCarthy might truly become the nominee.

Lyndon Johnson also read the election returns and understood. At 9 p.m. on the evening of March 31, the President addressed 70 million Americans over TV: "I am taking the first step to de-escalate the conflict," he said. "I have ordered our aircraft . . . to make no attacks on North Vietnam, except in the area [immediately] north of the Demilitarized Zone." This news was sensation enough. But the real shocker was still to come. "There is division in the American house now," said Johnson. "Accordingly I shall not seek, and I will not accept, the nomination of my party for another term as your President." The Vietnam war had toppled the President, who had started his 1964 term with the greatest majority of popular votes in history.

But the homefront battling over Vietnam was not over. When the Democrats convened in Chicago to pick a Presidential candidate in August, they faced the ticklish task of disowning a war that its leader once had wholeheartedly embraced. In a bitter convention, carried out against a bloody backdrop of street fights between peace demonstrators and Chicago police, Johnson's hand-picked candidate, Vice President Hubert Humphrey, was selected to lead the ticket. Shortly before, at a notably bland convention in Miami, the Republicans had chosen Richard Nixon. In the tight race that followed, neither man seemed willing to take a strong stand either for ending the war or for renewing escalation. Yet movies of Chicago police beating the antiwar demonstrators, shown all over the nation, probably helped to deprive Humphrey of the Presidency; he lost to Nixon by a mere 0.65 per cent of the vote.

Even in victory, Nixon, too, could understand the returns. Once a Hawk, he had advocated bombing the Reds in Indochina as far back as 1954. Now, 14 years later, he appeared to be closing the door on an era by promising to quit Vietnam. On June 8, 1969, he announced the withdrawal of 25,000 U.S. troops. Within a year, he had pledged to pull out 235,000 more by mid-1971. Though at decade's end there was grim evidence that the war was spreading into neighboring Laos and Cambodia, nevertheless, the reduced commitment within Vietnam itself suggested that the stiffening mood of the Doves might result in a long-range reduction of U.S. involvement in Asia.

225

Muscular Tycoons

Mickey Mantle, $100,000-a-year man, at spring training in 1967.

The Athlete as Entrepreneur

When I went up to the majors, the guys sat around reading the sports pages. Now they read the "Wall Street Journal."

NEW YORK YANKEES PITCHER WHITEY FORD

Two years before he made the above observation, the distinguished left-hander Whitey Ford saddened a generation of Yankee fans by announcing that he would give up his pitching job. However, in a departure from the old carpetbagging days when a typical sports-page-reading hero usually retired to the dreary shallows of bartending or chicken farming, when Ford finally walked out of the Yankee dugout for the last time he moved into the $50,000-a-year vice-presidency of a slick new concern called Trans National Communications, Inc. Trans National was a conglomerate that recorded pop music, controlled 100 radio stations, ran a truck farm in Florida and owned the Oakland Seals hockey team. Ford's partners were also athletes—Jim Katcavage, Pat Summerall and Dick Lynch—all late of the New York Giants football team, but now up to their burly shoulders in entrepreneuring. "Guess what?" said Lynch, one morning in 1969. "We just bought a bank."

Indeed they had. And this fancy financial coup by Lynch and Ford and company offered just the latest example of the kind of money that famous athletes were grabbing as professional sports soared ahead of the rest of the booming U.S. economy. Major-league franchises proliferated like gerbils, until nearly every sizable city in the country had gone big league in *something*. Television ads more than doubled the income of leagues and team owners, rookies signed for bonuses five times higher than Babe Ruth's income in his greatest year, and athletes in all the major sports learned to sell their names in new lines of business with a keen eye for profits.

By 1969 major-league baseball, which only nine years before had numbered 16 teams that drew an annual total of 16.1 million people, had ballooned to 24 teams with an attendance of 27.2 million. Between 1967 and 1969 the National Hockey League doubled in size to 12 teams. Pro basketball, which in the '50s had been a makeshift road show, found itself with 25 clubs in two rival leagues. All these sports were outstripped by professional football, whose National Football League expanded in 1967 to 16 teams and then began to swallow the upstart eight-team American Football League in a merger agreement that cost the American's owners a reported $18 million in indemnities. Within four years, pro football's

Battered but rich, $400,000 bonus baby Joe Namath quenches his thirst during the Jets' victorious 1969 Super Bowl game.

Jack Nicklaus

One of the longest hitters in golf, Nicklaus rivaled Palmer as the professional circuit's leading money-winner of the decade, earning $971,816 before he was 30 years old.

Sandy Koufax

Pitcher Koufax was paid $125,000 a season by Los Angeles when arthritis ended his career in 1966. He then signed a one-million-dollar contract as a sports commentator.

Willie Shoemaker

From 1951 through 1969, four-foot eleven-inch Shoemaker brought home more than $100,000 a year as the nation's top jockey. His biggest boodle: $3,052,146 in 1967.

Lew Alcindor

Upon graduation from U.C.L.A. in 1969, seven-foot two-inch Alcindor received more than one million dollars for signing to play for the Milwaukee Bucks for five years.

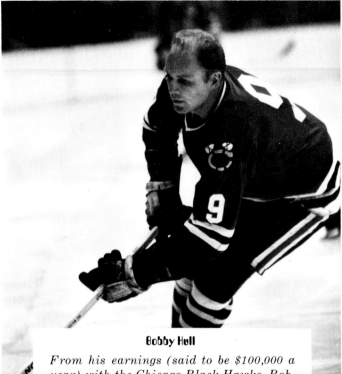

Bobby Hull

From his earnings (said to be $100,000 a year) with the Chicago Black Hawks, Bobby Hull built up a cattle enterprise of four ranches and 540 head in Ontario, Canada.

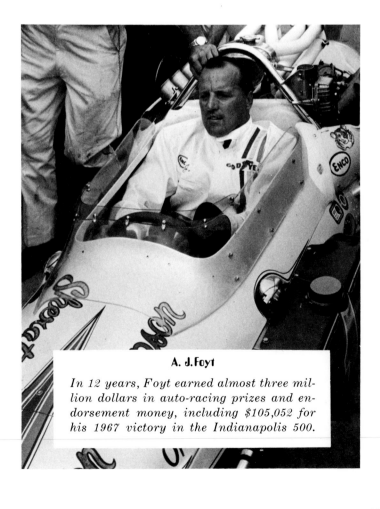

A. J. Foyt

In 12 years, Foyt earned almost three million dollars in auto-racing prizes and endorsement money, including $105,052 for his 1967 victory in the Indianapolis 500.

suave commissioner, Pete Rozelle, had signed the CBS, NBC *and* ABC networks to contracts that by 1974 would bring in the stupefying total of $142 million, a figure that prompted Clint Murchison, the oil zillionaire who owned the Dallas Cowboys, to describe Rozelle as "the greatest salesman in the history of the world."

Rozelle, however, was not the only one who realized he had something very hot to sell. The era of expansion and merger bred an atmosphere of interclub and interleague rivalry for talented young athletes that sent the price of sports livestock soaring. In the hard-rock times of 1950, the average salary of a big-league baseball player was about $10,000, football $8,200, basketball a scrabbly $7,000. Although a very few top baseball stars, such as the slugging outfielder Ted Williams of the Boston Red Sox, pulled down $100,000, even these titans had virtually nothing in the way of outside interests. "1938 was my big year," recalled Mel Hein, speaking of his off-field income in the days when, as all-pro center for the New York Giants, he earned less than $200 per game. "I got $150 for endorsing Mayflower Doughnuts. When I won the Most Valuable Player award, some pipe company sent me a set of pipes. Free!"

In the new, big-money era of the '60s, fresh-faced college boys retained lawyers and agents to exploit the bidding rivalries, then sat tight without so much as deigning to try on their rookie uniforms. In 1960, when the AFL was offering its first tentative challenge to the NFL, Louisiana State All-America halfback Billy Cannon boldly signed with a team in each league and then let the courts decide who owned him. He was eventually awarded to Houston in the AFL, which gave him a $100,000 bonus plus a string of gasoline stations for joining the team. In 1965 show business tycoon Sonny Werblin, who had bought the impoverished New York Titans and was trying to reconstruct them into a profit-making enterprise rechristened the Jets, laid out an estimated $427,000 for a swinging quarterback from the University of Alabama named Joe Namath. And one year later the Atlanta Falcons came up with $600,000 for University of Texas linebacker Tommy Nobis. "We're making millionaires," wailed coach and general manager Al Davis of the Oakland Raiders, "out of kids who can't even graduate." But powered by such youngsters as Nobis, Atlanta beat veteran clubs like New York and St. Louis in its very first season. And Namath's superb talents lifted the Jets from a bankrupt joke to a world championship team that grossed some three million dollars for the 1969 season.

The enticements for the athletes went beyond salary. When the University of Southern California's running back O.J. Simpson got ready to turn pro he demanded of the Buffalo Bills a three-year, $600,000 contract plus "a very substantial fringe benefit," which was interpreted as a slice of the team's profits. Moreover, O.J. figured he could triple his income by cashing in on the scores of opportunities for movies, TV, books and testimonials.

In basketball Lew Alcindor, the seven-foot two-inch, cat-quick center from U.C.L.A., was tempted by an offer of 3,500 head of cattle nicely accommodated on a 40,000-acre ranch all his own if he would play in the American Basketball Association. And, of course, one million dollars for signing and playing. But Alcindor signed instead with Milwaukee of the rival NBA, presumably for a richer arrangement. Other basketball players found even more ingenious ways to make money. When Rick Barry, the established star of the San Francisco Warriors, failed to get what he asked for in 1967, he jumped to the Oakland Oaks of the rival league for a $200,000 contract, plus a reported 15 per cent interest in the club. And in 1970 he became an ancillary package in the 11 million dollar indemnity the NBA demanded when the two leagues began to talk about a merger.

But the most eye-stopping bonanza was yielded up to Connie Hawkins, an ABA superstar who had been

232

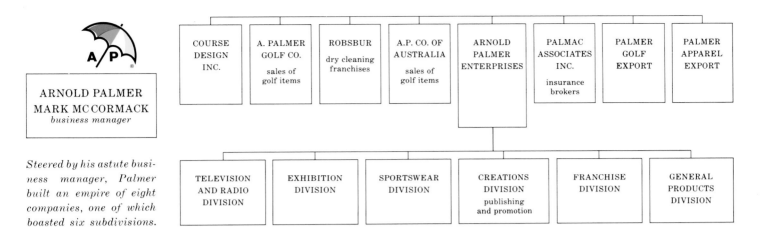

ARNOLD PALMER
MARK McCORMACK
business manager

COURSE DESIGN INC.

A. PALMER GOLF CO.
sales of golf items

ROBSBUR
dry cleaning franchises

A.P. CO. OF AUSTRALIA
sales of golf items

ARNOLD PALMER ENTERPRISES

PALMAC ASSOCIATES INC.
insurance brokers

PALMER GOLF EXPORT

PALMER APPAREL EXPORT

TELEVISION AND RADIO DIVISION

EXHIBITION DIVISION

SPORTSWEAR DIVISION

CREATIONS DIVISION
publishing and promotion

FRANCHISE DIVISION

GENERAL PRODUCTS DIVISION

Steered by his astute business manager, Palmer built an empire of eight companies, one of which boasted six subdivisions.

Golf millionaire Arnold Palmer, watched by a segment of his army of admirers, blasts out of a trap in the 1968 British Open.

avoided by the NBA because he was suspected of some undefined connection with a bribe when in college. He brought suit against the NBA, which gave him one million dollars for dropping the suit and signing up to play in their league after all. Said Jim Murray of the *Los Angeles Times*, after covering almost a decade of league-jumping, double-signing and militant agentry: "It seems these days that it takes a law degree to become a sports writer."

In the litigious, high-flying decade of the '60s, however, it was neither a league-jumper like Rick Barry nor a swinger like Joe Namath who scored the biggest financial victory. Rather it was a modest, friendly man named Arnold Palmer, the leading money winner ($1,388,619) in professional golf and kingpin of a business conglomerate greater than that operated by any other athlete in all the history of sport. Everything that Palmer did on a golf course was dramatic. He won spectacularly, making impossible recovery shots in the last few holes. He also lost spectacularly, blowing a sure win of $25,000 by missing a short putt on the final green. And it was an odd fact that Palmer always seemed to make his best and worst showings before the TV cameras. This instinct for big-league theatrics was no surprise to Palmer's wife, Winnie. "Whether he knows it or not," she said, "Arn is an actor."

Palmer cashed in on his electrifying star quality in a prodigious way. Under the shrewd guidance of his friend and business manager Mark McCormack, Palmer profitably lent his name to an empire of enterprises, endorsements and franchises. Prospective clients might blanch at some of Palmer's rock-bottom asking prices ($30,000 for a dry cleaning franchise). But McCormack had a compelling argument: "Regardless of what you pay for Arnold Palmer, it would be much less than what you would have to pay to build a brand name from the beginning. Arnold Palmer *is* a brand name."

And so he was. At one time or another during the decade, a fan could not only learn to play golf with Palmer clubs, dress in Palmer regalia (made in the U.S., Canada, New Zealand, Hong Kong, Australia, France, South Africa and Japan); he could also stay in a Palmer motel or buy a Palmer lot to build a house on. He could trim his grass with a Palmer-approved lawnmower or do home carpentry with Palmer-endorsed power tools. He could buy insurance from a Palmer agency, be served by a Palmer maid, shave with Palmer lather, spray on Palmer deodorant, swig a Palmer soft drink, eat a Palmer candy bar, smoke Palmer's preferred cigarette, fly with his favorite airline and, for about $750,000, buy a corporate plane just like Palmer's own, a Jet Commander. All told, his brand-name concerns produced for Arnie an annual income that went into the high six figures, not even counting his golf winnings, which averaged $150,000. In 1966 the firms in which Palmer had a direct or licensing interest reported sales close to $15 million, and Arnold's own companies had an annual payroll of some $750,000.

No other single athlete came close to matching Palmer's fantastic business success, though many *(opposite)* gave it a hefty try. They sang, acted, announced sports events, and owned or promoted nightclubs, real estate, brokerage houses and take-out food franchises. Many appeared in mod ads selling travel, resorts and even lines of perfume said to be perfectly all right for manly men.

Viewing all this tycoonery as the decade drew to a close, sportswriter Steve Cady summed up the fascination of the fans as they watched their heroes play at the new game of big business: "In less complicated times, a champion fighter used to mumble through bloodied teeth, 'I'd just like to say hello to my mother. Hi, ma. I'm fine.' Nowadays, star athletes reaching the microphone would be more apt to say: 'I'd just like to say hello to my attorney, my business partner, my ancillary adviser, my theatrical agent and my publisher. Hi, boys. We're doing fine.'"

Money on the Side

*Dozens of pros fell in step with stars
like Mantle and Namath and went into business. Here is a
sampling of players and their outside interests.*

LANCE ALWORTH
Wide Receiver, San Diego Chargers
JANTZEN INC. sportswear
endorsement
60 MINUTE CLEANERS
dry cleaning franchise
VENTURE HAIR CREAM
endorsement

YOGI BERRA
Coach, New York Mets
YOOHOO chocolate drink, part owner

JIM BROWN
Fullback, Cleveland Browns
DESENEX foot powder, endorsement
THE DIRTY DOZEN, movie actor

STEIN ERICKSON
Skier
SCHLITZ BEER, endorsement

ROMAN GABRIEL
Quarterback, Los Angeles Rams
GABRIEL AND OLSON
TRAVEL AGENCY
GABRIEL AND OLSON
VOLKSWAGEN AGENCY

ROCKY GRAZIANO
Boxer
DANNON YOGURT, endorsement
HAMM'S beer, endorsement
PIZZA RING, restaurant franchise

VIC HADFIELD
Left Wing, New York Rangers
MC GREGOR sportswear, endorsement

GORDIE HOWE
Right Wing, Detroit Red Wings
CALDERONE-CURRAN
RANCHES INC., part owner
GORDON HOWE PROMOTION
AGENCY INC., part owner

"**What right
have we got
running an
employment
agency?**"

"Our people
are pros,   just like us."

Mantle Men & Namath Girls, Inc.

BRADY KEYS
Defensive Back, Pittsburgh Steelers
ALL-PRO CHICKEN
restaurant franchise

VINCE LOMBARDI
Coach, Washington Redskins
NESTLE'S QUICK
chocolate drink, endorsement
STATE FARM INSURANCE
COMPANIES, endorsement

MICKEY MANTLE
Outfielder, New York Yankees
COUNTRY COOKIN' INC.
restaurant franchise
EDWARDS & HANLY, endorsement

GINO MARCHETTI
Defensive End, Baltimore Colts
GINO'S PIZZA, restaurant franchise

JOE NAMATH
Quarterback, New York Jets
BACHELORS III, Boston
restaurant, part owner
BROADWAY JOE'S
restaurant franchise
SCHICK ELECTRIC INC.
endorsement

TOM SEAVER
Pitcher, New York Mets
CAESAR'S PALACE, Las Vegas
personal appearance
EASTMAN KODAK COMPANY
public relations
ELECTRONIC COMPUTER
PROGRAMMING INSTITUTE
endorsement

O. J. SIMPSON
Running Back, Buffalo Bills
CHEVROLET, endorsement
EASTMAN KODAK COMPANY
public relations

Y. A. TITTLE
Quarterback, New York Giants
TITTLE, IVERSON, PURCELL,
JONES AND SCURRY INSURANCE
COMPANY
insurance brokers, part owner

BOBBY UNSER
Auto Racer
WINNING, movie actor

JERRY WEST
Guard, Los Angeles Lakers
PEPSI-COLA, Sports Staff Board

MAURY WILLS
Infielder, Los Angeles Dodgers
STOLEN BASE BANJO CLUB
restaurant franchise
STOLEN BASE CLEANERS
dry cleaning franchise

Singles

Young Chicagoans in Butch's, a singles bar.

The Young Unmarrieds

Norms of mate selections—as sociologists rather coarsely phrase it—can be looked at as a classification of social groups in some of which marriage is to be preferred and in others is to be avoided.

PROFESSOR JOHN FINLEY SCOTT, UNIVERSITY OF WASHINGTON

"Marriage?" said Janet Hyland, a youthful schoolteacher in Los Angeles. "Oh, not yet. I haven't had nearly enough of a whirl yet." This confident girl was in many ways typical of the young unmarrieds of the '60s. They were an independent lot. Many, like Janet, had moved from small towns to cities to seek glamorous or challenging jobs. And they were affluent. In 1967 eight million young singles earned over $50 billion, much of which they spent on dating.

The exploitation of this lucrative market had its organized beginnings in 1962, when Grossinger's Hotel *(page 252)* in the Catskills ran a singles-only weekend, the first such promotion on record. Soon the singles were being served by many shrewd entrepreneurs. One was Mike O'Harro *(right)*, who got into the business when, as an ensign marooned in Arlington, Virginia, in 1964, he threw a party for other singles as lonely as he was. Within three years, Mike had built up a 47,000-member club, JOPA (Junior Officers and Professional Association), whose million-dollar operation financed singles ventures in travel and entertainment.

By the late '60s, a whole singles subculture had emerged. There were singles-only resorts, singles-only publications and singles-only apartment houses. Planeloads of singles toured Europe, and the ocean liner *Olympia* took singles cruises to the Bahamas. Every night hordes of young swingers shoehorned into singles bars and struck up chumships with total strangers of the opposite sex. In New York their rendezvous included Friday's and Mr. Laffs. Chicago had The Store, San Francisco boasted Paoli's, and Dallas the TGIF (Thank God It's Friday).

Some aspects of this dating game were sad or downright unpleasant. Of the singles bars, a stewardess said in disgust, "It's a zoo scene. Everyone just wants to grab you." Some women, desperate to trap a husband, became joyless profligates in what psychiatrist Judianne Densen-Gerber described as a "search for an answer to loneliness that just breeds more loneliness." However, one singles businessman, Steve Milgrim, pointed out that unhappiness was an old, old story and that the modern dating game could not be expected to solve everyone's hang-up. He declared philosophically, "You bring *some* happiness to *some* people, the whole thing becomes worthwhile."

Hosting a profitable party in Washington, D.C., Mike O'Harro stamps a girl's hand to show she paid her three-dollar fee.

Ads promoting singles activities offer "incredible friendships." One club's cryptic rule: "All female members must be female."

Computer Courtship

"We just wanted to take some of the blindness out of blind dating." This was the aim of Operation Match, one of hundreds of computerized dating agencies that sprang up to serve the booming singles market of the '60s. By 1967, after only two years in business, Operation Match claimed to have put 130,000 singles (out of five million clients) on the road to wedded bliss, including the three couples pictured here.

Although the service of these computer-dating companies was based on advanced electronic technology, the actual date-making was really quite simple. A client received and filled out questionnaires like the preliminary one at right, sketching in his background, attitudes and tastes. The results were then coded on a punch card, which was matched with others by a computer. When close match-ups were found, indicating compatible personalities, the agency arranged for an introduction—in fact, as many as a customer might want (at prices ranging from $20 for 24 to 48 names, to $495 for five years' service). Mel Zander *(right, above)* had six computerized dates before he drew Judy Fast, who became his bride. Of course logical match-ups did not guarantee congenial dates, as the letter below testifies.

However, other computer matches came through loud and clear on the first electronic contact. One perfect match-up was Benson Lee, a Chinese-American engineer, and Vicki Lindquist, a Pennsylvania Quaker. Both loved sports cars, owned hi-fi sets and had actually assembled them. And both worked for the same company—IBM, the computer manufacturer.

Dear Gentlemen: Your computer was right. Mitzi W. and I like all the same things. It is truly remarkable. We like the same food, we both like the opera. Mitzi likes bike riding and so do I. Actually, there was only one thing we didn't like—each other. Dwight J.

Computer spouses: the Zanders (top), the Lees, the Feins.

COMPATIBILITY'S PERSONALITY INVENTORY

Please give your first spontaneous reaction to each of the following questions. If you strongly agree with the statement, circle 1, if you agree, circle 2, if you neither agree nor disagree, circle 3, if you disagree, circle 4 if you strongly disagree with the statement, circle 5. Although it may be hard to decide on some questions, be sure to answer all of them.

	Agree		?	Disagree	
1. My parents were fairly religious and so am I.	1	2	3	4	5
2. Religious convictions help produce a home that is harmonious and stable.	1	2	3	4	5
3. I believe in God.	1	2	3	4	5
4. I attend church regularly and would prefer a mate who does the same.	1	2	3	4	5
5. Parents who do not provide religious training for their children are not fulfilling their responsibilities	1	2	3	4	5
6. I believe in the existence of a Supreme Being that controls the fate of mankind.	1	2	3	4	5
7. The breakdown of organized religion is a major problem in our society today.	1	2	3	4	5
8. My religious faith has helped me understand the difference between right and wrong.	1	2	3	4	5
9. A fine moral code can be a good substitute for a religious code.	1	2	3	4	5
10. A person can have high moral standards without being religious.	1	2	3	4	5
11. The portrayal of sex in the movies has gone too far.	1	2	3	4	5
12. I believe that married women who work desert their home for a career.	1	2	3	4	5
13. It is not appropriate to include sex education in the school program.	1	2	3	4	5
14. It is the parents' obligation and responsibility to tell their youth how to dress.	1	2	3	4	5
15. Long hair and beards are a sign of the breakdown in our society.	1	2	3	4	5
16. Current obscenity laws, covering magazines and books, are not strong enough.	1	2	3	4	5
17. Years ago people had more fun than they do today.	1	2	3	4	5
18. I frequently seek new and exciting experiences.	1	2	3	4	5
19. Children must learn when they are very young deep respect for law and order.	1	2	3	4	5
20. Students and children must accept the basic authority of parents and teachers.	1	2	3	4	5
21. I usually feel ill at ease at large parties.	1	2	3	4	5
22. I belong to many different kinds of clubs and organizations.	1	2	3	4	5
23. People who know me describe me as friendly and outgoing.	1	2	3	4	5
24. It is rather easy for me to make new friends.	1	2	3	4	5
25. I am likely to confide in my friends and share my feelings with them.	1	2	3	4	5
26 I would rather do things with others than by myself.	1	2	3	4	5
27. I am more a listener and a follower than a leader.	1	2	3	4	5
28. I often am happier doing something at a home than going to a party.	1	2	3	4	5
29. I enjoy mixing with many different kinds of people.	1	2	3	4	5
30. I often like to spend time by myself.	1	2	3	4	5
31. I am affectionate and express my feelings easily.	1	2	3	4	5
32. Young people today are basically right in their attitudes toward sex.	1	2	3	4	5
33. The importance of sex to a successful marriage has been overstressed.	1	2	3	4	5
34. There is no place for sex outside of marriage.	1	2	3	4	5
35. I tend to like people who easily display their affection.	1	2	3	4	5
36. There is too much discussion of sex today.	1	2	3	4	5
37. I consider myself to be a passionate person.	1	2	3	4	5
38. Mutual respect is much more important than sex in a successful marriage.	1	2	3	4	5
39. It is not proper for people to display their emotions in public.	1	2	3	4	5
40. People should not tell sexy jokes at parties.	1	2	3	4	5
41. People who know me tend to see me as fairly excitable.	1	2	3	4	5
42. I tend to be fairly tense.	1	2	3	4	5
43. I easily fly off the handle.	1	2	3	4	5
44. I rarely get into arguments.	1	2	3	4	5
45. I often feel guilty.	1	2	3	4	5
46. My feelings are easily hurt.	1	2	3	4	5
47. I am considered to be calm and collected.	1	2	3	4	5
48. I am prone to act before I think.	1	2	3	4	5
49. I am much more optimistic than pessimistic.	1	2	3	4	5
50. I am generally good natured and cheerful.	1	2	3	4	5

This is not an inventory to assess personal problems. It is only intended to ascertain interests and attitudes in some areas considered to be important in interpersonal compatibility.

NAME_____ADDRESS_____CITY_____ZIP_____

AGE_____SEX_____HOME PHONE_____WORK PHONE_____OCCUPATION_____

© 1969, INTERNATIONAL COMPATIBILITY, INC.   LAT 11/9

A computer dating service form tested views on sex, religion and child rearing. Most clients avoided extreme answers.

Swingers of both sexes mingle outside Friday's, one of a dozen crowded singles bars on Manhattan's Upper East Side.

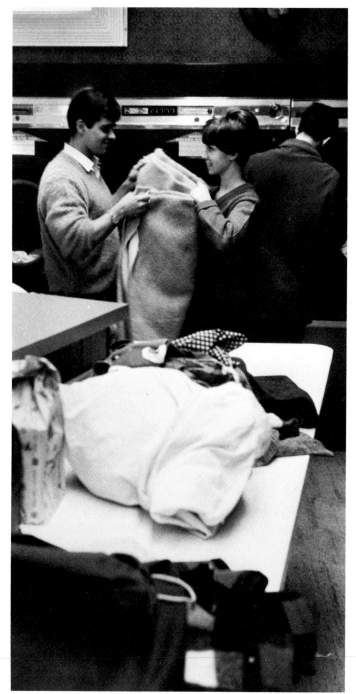

Friendly Chicagoans fold a blanket in a local laundromat.

Where the Boys—and Girls—Are

The ultimate setup for young unmarrieds was the singles-only apartment complex, formally described in promoters' parlance as a "residential-recreational community for single young adults." The printed ads for such promising pleasure-domes were less restrained: "Come live where the fun is," said one puff. Part of the fun in a typical singles complex could be had from such facilities as swimming pools, gymnasiums, tennis courts and indoor golfing ranges. But the greatest lure was guaranteed proximity to the opposite sex. For tonight's date—and possibly tomorrow's spouse—might be no farther away than the next-door buzzer.

Not surprisingly, these self-contained communities blossomed first in California, long a hotbed of grandiose promotions and novel life styles. In 1965, three young real-estate men, taking careful note of the success of another birds-of-a-feather real-estate venture, the local retirement village *(pages 116-127)*, formed an apartment-building corporation called the South Bay Club and broke ground in Torrance for the first singles enclave. Even before the construction was finished, every one of its 248 apartment units had been rented. By 1970 the club had 13 complexes, including one in Phoenix, Arizona; they totaled some 6,000 individual apartment units with more than 8,000 tenants, and still other large complexes were planned. Meanwhile another real-estate outfit had built three thriving communities in the Los Angeles area: the 130-unit Friday Apartments in North Torrance, the 200-unit Friday Sylmar in Sylmar and the 143-unit Friday U.S.A. in South Torrance *(right)*.

The singles who answered this clarion call to frolic and friendship were cut to a distinct pattern. They

A prospective tenant studies a floor plan.

ranged in age from 21 to 40, and worked at respectable white-collar professions. Their average income of $8,000 gave them ample wherewithal to manage the monthly rents, which ranged upward from $120 for a one-room apartment with bath and kitchenette. Though generally well-informed and fairly sophisticated, they had a massive disinterest in the new-wave radicalism that had swept across the country. "This," said Howard Ruby, one of the founding fathers of the South Bay Club, "is the America you don't hear about. It's clean-cut people who don't wear sandals and beards—guys and girls living very normal lives. It's almost blasphemous how American it is."

Singles who signed on for this Middle-American adventure found themselves caught up in a whirl of group activities, planned in some complexes by full-time resident social directors. In the South Bay Club chain, there were barbecues, costume balls, wine tastings, bridge tournaments, "Las Vegas Gambling Nights" and "New England Corned Beef Dinners." One building held round-table discussions on every subject from birth control to the John Birch Society. When all else failed, a restless resident could always find someone to talk to. A door left ajar was an open invitation to chat. If several neighbors happened by, an impromptu party was the usual result.

There was, of course, one problem for singles-apartment dwellers: those who wed were politely asked to find new quarters. Though a typical complex lost eight or nine tenants to marriage in a year, this represented no permanent loss to the management. For each outcast newlywed, there was a waiting list of eager applicants clamoring to make the scene.

A split-level beer party runs long into the night at Friday U.S.A., a singles-only apartment complex in Torrance, California.

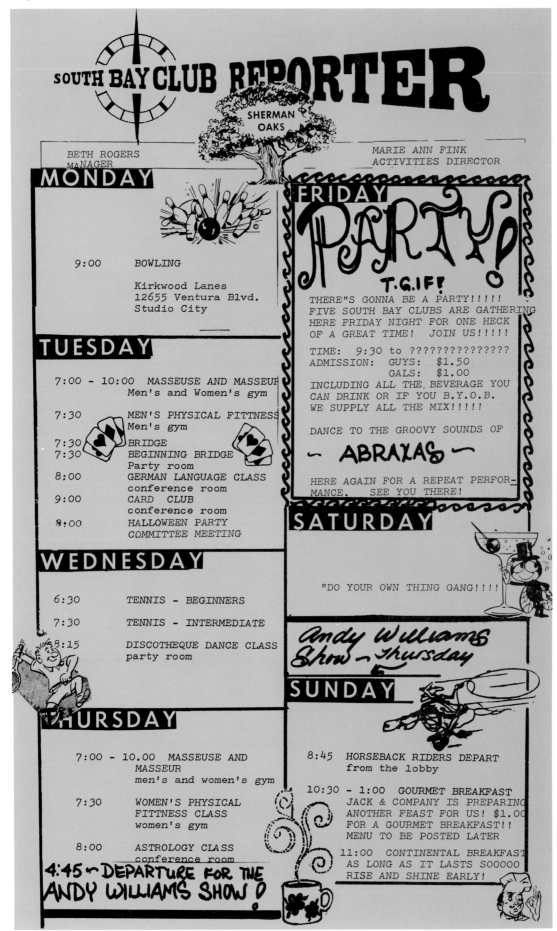

SOUTH BAY CLUB REPORTER

SHERMAN OAKS

BETH ROGERS
MANAGER

MARIE ANN FINK
ACTIVITIES DIRECTOR

MONDAY

9:00   BOWLING

Kirkwood Lanes
12655 Ventura Blvd.
Studio City

TUESDAY

7:00 - 10:00 MASSEUSE AND MASSEUR
Men's and Women's gym

7:30   MEN'S PHYSICAL FITTNESS
Men's gym

7:30   BRIDGE
7:30   BEGINNING BRIDGE
Party room

8:00   GERMAN LANGUAGE CLASS
conference room

9:00   CARD CLUB
conference room

8:00   HALLOWEEN PARTY
COMMITTEE MEETING

WEDNESDAY

6:30   TENNIS - BEGINNERS

7:30   TENNIS - INTERMEDIATE

8:15   DISCOTHEQUE DANCE CLASS
party room

THURSDAY

7:00 - 10.00 MASSEUSE AND
MASSEUR
men's and women's gym

7:30   WOMEN'S PHYSICAL
FITTNESS CLASS
women's gym

8:00   ASTROLOGY CLASS
conference room

4:45 ~ DEPARTURE FOR THE
ANDY WILLIAMS SHOW!

FRIDAY

PARTY!

T.G.IF!

THERE"S GONNA BE A PARTY!!!!!
FIVE SOUTH BAY CLUBS ARE GATHERING
HERE FRIDAY NIGHT FOR ONE HECK
OF A GREAT TIME! JOIN US!!!!!

TIME: 9:30 to ???????????????
ADMISSION: GUYS: $1.50
            GALS: $1.00
INCLUDING ALL THE, BEVERAGE YOU
CAN DRINK OR IF YOU B.Y.O.B.
WE SUPPLY ALL THE MIX!!!!!

DANCE TO THE GROOVY SOUNDS OF

~ ABRAXAS ~

HERE AGAIN FOR A REPEAT PERFOR-
MANCE.   SEE YOU THERE!

SATURDAY

"DO YOUR OWN THING GANG!!!!

Andy Williams
Show ~ Thursday

SUNDAY

8:45   HORSEBACK RIDERS DEPART
from the lobby

10:30 - 1:00 GOURMET BREAKFAST
JACK & COMPANY IS PREPARING
ANOTHER FEAST FOR US! $1.00
FOR A GOURMET BREAKFAST!!
MENU TO BE POSTED LATER

11:00   CONTINENTAL BREAKFAST
AS LONG AS IT LASTS SOOOOO
RISE AND SHINE EARLY!

The bulletin of a South Bay Club singles complex lists the week's events.

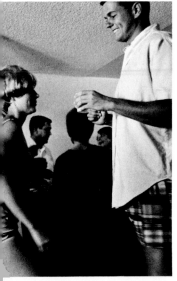

Tenants begin an ad-lib dance.

A girl chats with next-door neighbors as she does her ironing.

South Bay Club tenants throw a party for visiting players of the Boston Patriots pro football team.

A beer-cooled piggyback fight delights a group of singles in the whirlpool of their Torrance, California, apartment house.

Cupid in the Catskills

In the Catskill Mountains of New York lies a concentration of resort hotels renowned for their homey hospitality, high-paid entertainers and kosher food. It was here in 1962 that the singles game was first played in big-league style when Grossinger's, a 1,200-bed institution, staged its first singles-only weekend. On a Friday evening in March, some 1,000 eager but nervous singles piled out of their buses and plunged into a strenuous schedule of skiing, hiking, dancing —and, of course, investigating guests of the opposite sex. Everyone loved it, and Grossinger's and its Catskill rivals were in the singles business to stay. For the male guests, usually outnumbered, it was a buyer's market; many a girl returned home with nothing on the hook. And yet other singles made a lasting connection, attested to in letters of thanks *(below)*.

Last summer I stayed at Grossinger's Hotel for the Fourth of July weekend and for the "Singles" week (July 7-14). I can honestly say that it was the most wonderful and memorable vacation I ever had; for that was the week Paul and I met each other and fell in love. In a way Paul and I feel indebted to you for the happiness we now share. To show our appreciation we would like to have you attend our wedding.

The last Sunday of a truly delightful week, Mitch and I met in the lobby. Two and a half years later, on Feb. 9, 1969, we were married.

I don't think you remember me, I was up to Grossinger's three years ago, for the singles weekend, August 21, and I met Irving. I thought you'd be happy to know, we were married and are very happy, thank God.

Thank you for being directly responsible for my happiness today. On July 7, 1968, I arrived for a Singles Week; that day I met Harvey. On August 10, 1969 we were married and are now blissfully happy. Thank you again—and long live Grossinger's Singles Weeks!

A slick pamphlet lists Grossinger's program for the week.

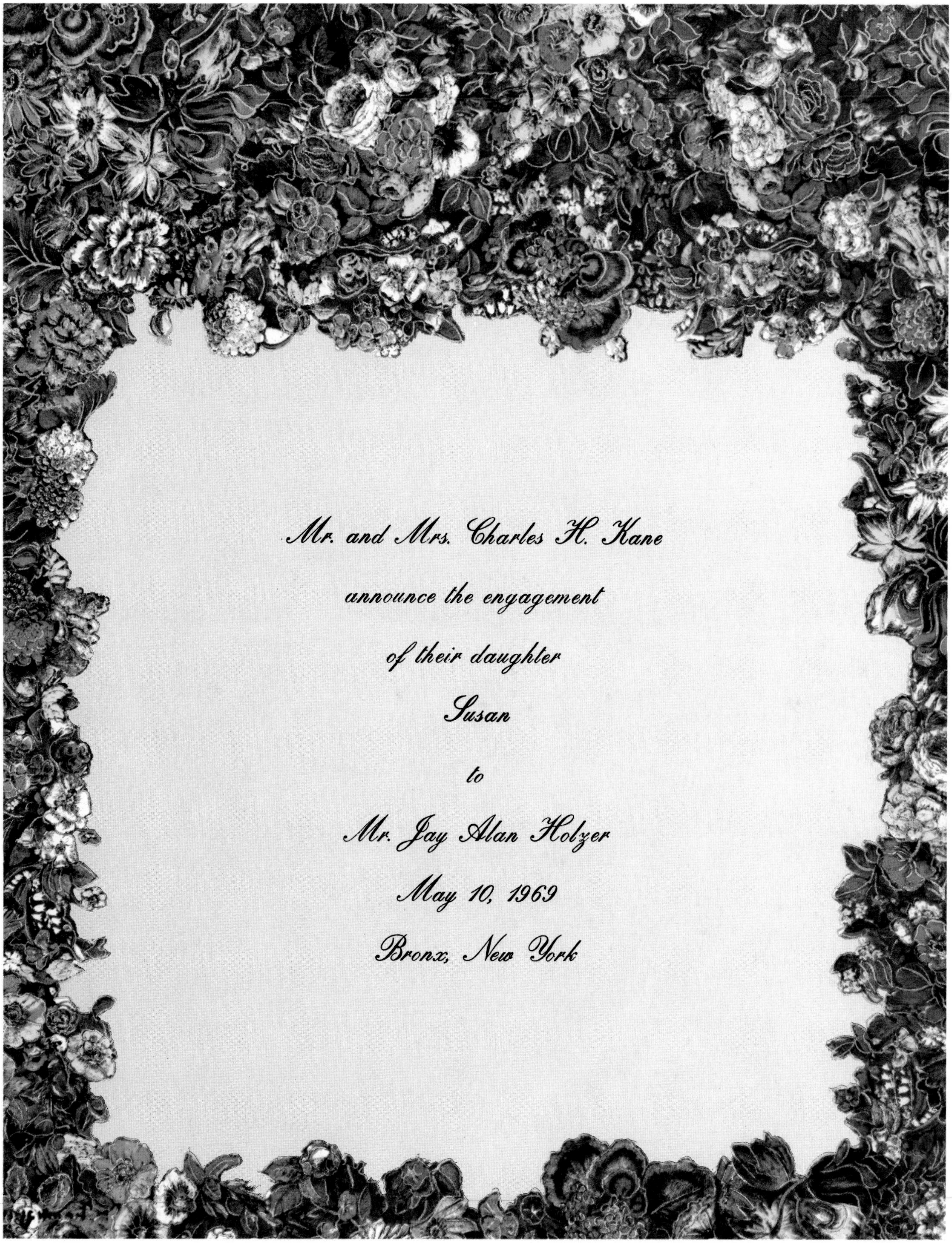

Mr. and Mrs. Charles H. Kane

announce the engagement

of their daughter

Susan

to

Mr. Jay Alan Holzer

May 10, 1969

Bronx, New York

New Yorker Susan Kane, who met her future mate at Grossinger's, gratefully sent the hotel an engagement announcement.

Science

The moon meets its conquerors, July 20, 1969.

Science Fiction Comes True

Across the gulf of centuries the blind smile of Homer is turned upon our age. For somewhere in the world today, still unconscious of his destiny, walks the boy who will be the first Odysseus of the Age of Space.

ARTHUR C. CLARKE, THE CHALLENGE OF THE SPACESHIP, 1959

"It's a pity that taxpayers don't read science fiction," noted Frederik Pohl in 1962. "They might know more about the age they're buying." A hint of resentment was contained in these words, because Pohl, a leading writer and editor in the field, knew that modern technology was stealing sci-fi ideas at an alarming rate. Despite a penchant for bug-eyed monsters and mechanical grotesqueries *(right)*, science fiction has always been good at prophecy. A pioneer of the genre, Hugo Gernsback, predicted radar in 1911; Arthur C. Clarke wrote of communications satellites in the '40s; and in 1944 one innocent science fiction prophet gave such an exact description of the atomic bomb, then under top-secret development at Los Alamos, that the FBI ran a frantic check on him to see if he was a spy.

But science made such headlong progress in the '60s that many congenital futurists began to wonder if they could stay ahead of the game. Technology was plagiarizing such staples of the sci-fi imagination as computers that could calculate millions of times faster than the human brain, laser beams to light up the moon, and vehicles to take man to the bottom of the oceans. Real-life scientists were actually trying to detect life elsewhere in the universe and learning how to manipulate genes to cure diseases and guide the course of evolution.

To get them through this trying period, fans of the far out could fall back on a number of still-unrealized schemes for galactic federations and entry into the fifth dimension via time-warp. However, their favorite fantasy—space flight—had to be relinquished to the matter-of-fact world. Back in the 1930s, space flight was the exclusive property of the pulp magazines and comic strips, read mainly by teen-age boys who exhibited a certain manic glaze over the eyes as they relished outlandish adventures among the planets. By the '60s it had all changed. In 1961 President Kennedy said that mankind would reach the moon by the end of the decade, and his prediction came true right on schedule. Sci-fi readers could take some consolation when John Glenn, the first American to orbit the earth, cited boyish curiosity as his main motivation for the trip ("I have never grown up," he said), but it was nonetheless disconcerting to see their finest dream dragged into the cold light of reality.

THE ELEMENTS OF SCIENCE-FICTION

A hodge-podge of technology, this creature from a 1953 sci-fi magazine has radar eyes, tanklike feet and a computer mind.

It was a strange vertebrated animal. Its dark purple head was dimly suggestive of a chameleon, but it had such a high forehead and such a braincase as no reptile ever displayed before; the vertical pitch of its face gave it a most extraordinary resemblance to a human being. At last this unknown creature of the abyss blinked its eyes open, and, shading them with its disengaged hand, opened its mouth and gave vent to a shouting noise, articulate almost as speech might be, that penetrated even the steel case and padded jacket of the sphere.

H. G. WELLS, *IN THE ABYSS*, 1896

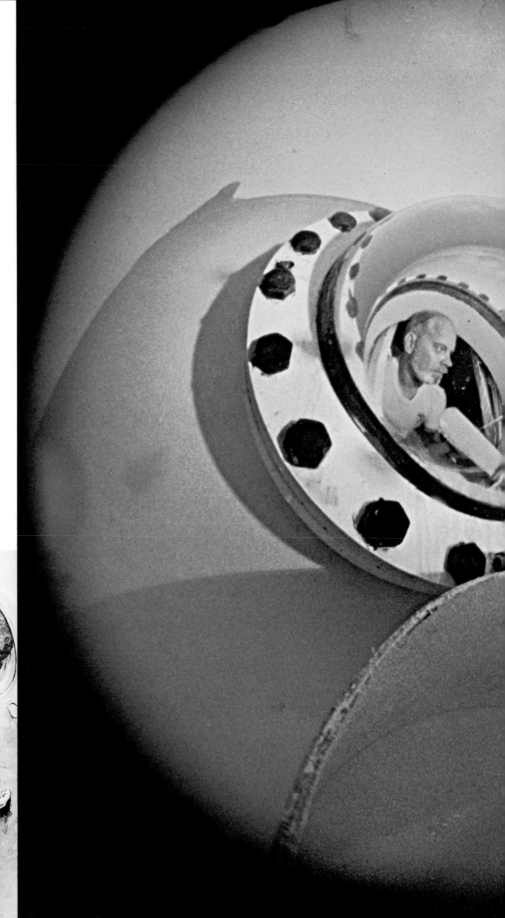

An H. G. Wells hero (pictured at left) saw intelligent undersea life; U.S. aquanauts who lived below for 60 days found none.

Under the Sea

H. G. Wells dreamed of cities full of manlike creatures on the ocean floor, and another science fiction pioneer, Jules Verne, wrote of a certain Captain Nemo who smoked seaweed cigars and coaxed oysters to produce giant pearls as he traveled 20,000 leagues under the sea. While real-life science of the '60s could not quite match such deeds, it was not for lack of trying.

At the start of the decade, less than 5 per cent of the earth's underwater terrain had been explored, and even by mid-decade scientists admitted that they knew more about the far side of the moon. To remedy this situation, dozens of deep-diving vessels burbled down to the sea bottom in the '60s seeking information on the currents, terrain, and eerie forms of life in the crushing deep. They found vast harvestable deposits of mineral ores, oil and gas.

Going a dramatic step beyond oceanic reconnoitering, Project Tektite *(left)* established a dormitory on the bottom of the Caribbean where aquanauts could study underwater ecology. By the end of the decade many scientists were predicting that sea farmers would someday operate out of such stations, cultivating plants and fish to feed the burgeoning population of the world. As President Kennedy said, "Knowledge of the oceans is more than a matter of curiosity. Our very survival may hinge upon it."

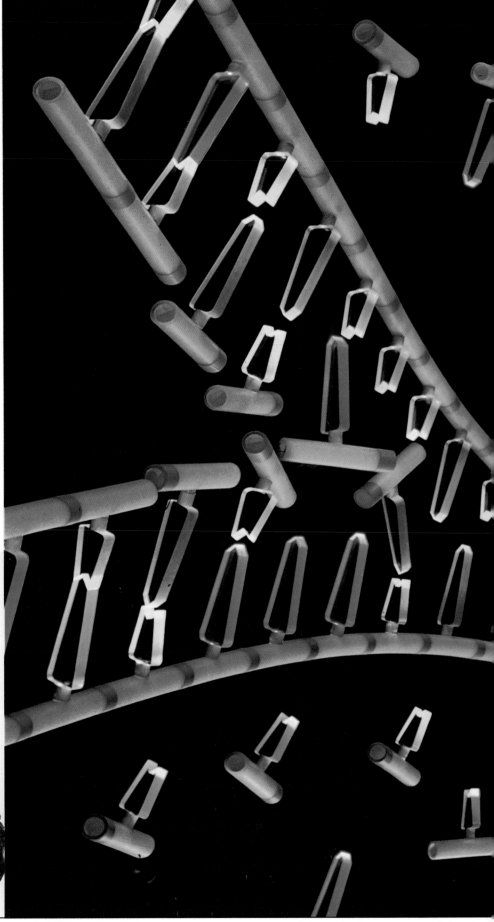

"I state facts," he began, by way of introduction. "Several months ago I began to experiment on living tissue with high-frequency, short-wavelength X-rays. By properly modulating the wavelengths of the rays sprayed upon the chromosomes, I found it possible to accelerate normal evolution or to retard it; to produce mutations—the creation of new species, such as mammals from reptiles—or to inhibit them. If we can control evolution; if we can hasten nature forward at the rate of a million years in one of our human years, who will profit? Is it worth perfecting? No one of us knows what perfection is."

JOHN TAINE, *SEEDS OF LIFE*, 1931

John Taine wrote of a mad genius who produced monsters by turning X-rays on the genetic material of life, shown above.

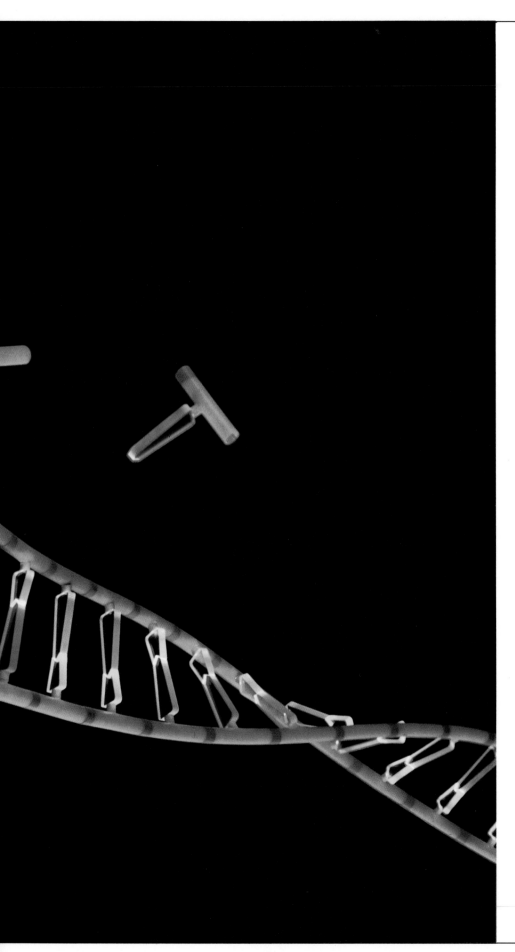

The Secret of Life

When tinkering with heredity, science fiction tends to summon up two-million-volt X-ray machines or at least to call in a deluge of radiation from some super-nova that has exploded nearby. But when three U.S. scientists — Marshall Nirenberg, Har Gobind Khorana and Robert Holley — actually succeeded in deciphering the genetic code between 1961 and 1965, they did it by painstaking chemical analysis of such lowly creatures as bacteria and viruses.

They already knew that the genetic controls of life are long molecules of DNA (easy-speak for deoxyribonucleic acid), which reside in the nuclei of cells. These talented molecules, resembling twisted ladders, can duplicate themselves by splitting apart, as shown at left. Every three rungs on the DNA ladder consists of a single chemical instruction for a part of a protein that will be manufactured by a cell, and many such instructions dictate whether an organism will grow into a giraffe, fern or man.

Nirenberg, Khorana and Holley learned how to read the triplet commands of DNA, and biochemists all over the world immediately began to search for ways of eliminating such genetic diseases as diabetes and hemophilia. No instant miracles were expected, for the genetic material in a human cell is awesomely complex, probably containing six billion rungs on its DNA ladders. But Dr. Nirenberg predicted that in 20 or 30 years geneticists will probably be able to rewrite the recipe for human beings.

*Addison watched in fascination
as the pilot maneuvered to get
the madman's ship on one of the
cross hairs. Suddenly the gunner
touched a button and the screen
was illuminated by a blinding
flash that left Addison's sight a
swimming pool of billowing after-
image. He blinked and looked
back, but their ship had leveled
off and he looked to another
screen where he found the enemy
circling and diving frantically
to get out of the way. He
was amazed to find that
the nose of their enemy was
strangely missing.*

    "What happened to them?"

    *"We cut off a section of the
prow with a molecule disrupter,"
the captain said absently.*

HENRIK DAHL JUVE
THE SILENT DESTROYER, 1929

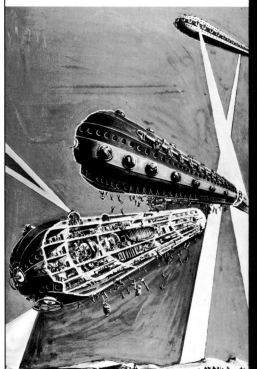

Almost as intense as Juve's 1929 energy ray, the concentrated light of a laser signaled to a satellite on the moon in 1968.

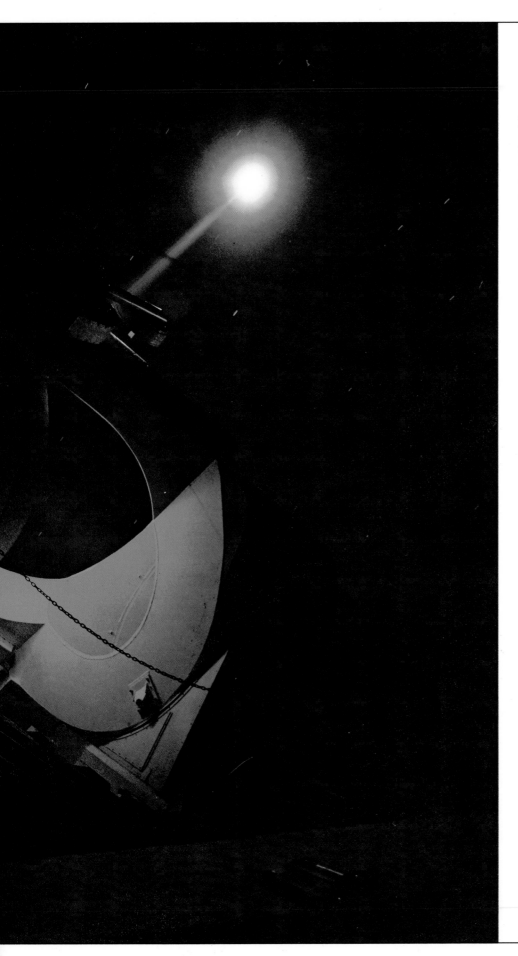

Laser Light

In 1960 a scientist at Hughes Aircraft Company in California built the first laser — an instrument that generates light waves of a single wavelength that are coherent (all in step). This gives them extraordinary properties; a pencil-thin laser beam can be enormously intense. Like the disintegrator rays of science fiction, laser light proved powerful enough to burn holes in diamonds or jab across the reaches of outer space. Soon it was being employed to cut metals, repair detached retinas, treat cancer, overcome the Stygian dark of the oceans and align such huge structures as bridges and dams.

Some of the most exciting laser experiments had to do with communications. A laser beam sent from Kitt Peak National Observatory in Arizona *(left)* was easily spotted by the television eye of the Surveyor 7 unmanned spacecraft on the moon. High-frequency laser light was also modulated to transmit messages; in theory, a single laser beam could carry all the radio, television and telephone communications of the world. In addition, it was discovered that laser light, aimed through a special kind of photographic image called a hologram, could project three-dimensional pictures which seemed to float in the air. By the end of the decade, scientists saw that in the laser they had a keystone to future technology.

The Brain was housed in an imposing structure in the center of the city. It had grown from a small beginning and was still growing, now occupying almost half a cubic mile with its millions of banks of selenium cells, thought records, contact switches, idea-association relays and a dozen other parts the very principles of which were beyond his understanding. From this brain was controlled, very literally controlled, the whole planet. Every city in the world had a relay station through which this central brain dictated its policies and determined its destiny.

LAURENCE MANNING
THE MAN WHO AWOKE, 1933

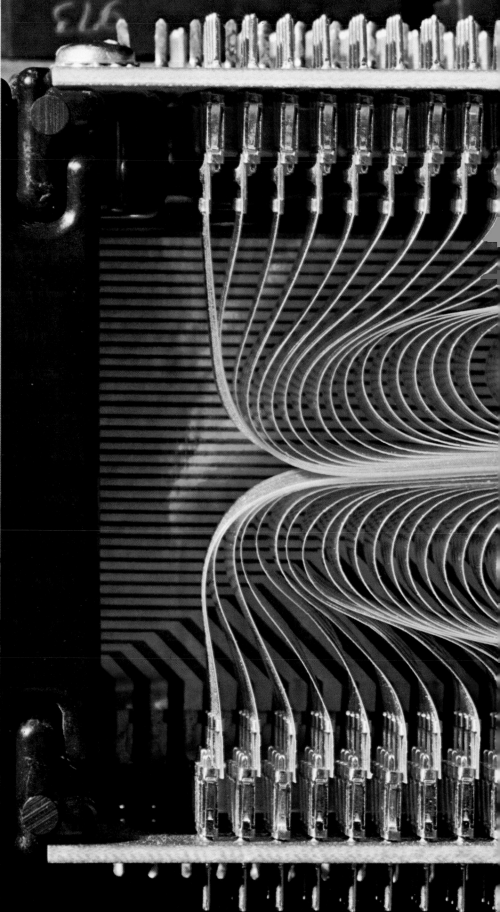

Unlike Laurence Manning's fiendish mechanical brain, the circuitry of an IBM 360 computer (above) is benignly brilliant.

The Computer Age

An oft-repeated joke of the '60s told of a scientist who asked a giant computer, "Is there a God?" The computer whirred and clicked for a moment, then replied, "There is now." While no computer of the decade actually exhibited such overweening pride, the machines could indeed calculate millions of times faster than their makers. They totted up bank accounts, routed telephone calls, set type, prepared weather forecasts, directed city traffic, dictated how sausages and ice cream were made, and guided astronauts through space.

Some engineers suggested dividing history into B.C. and A.C.—before and after computers. However, many citizens had good reasons to doubt the blessings of the computer age—as can be seen from the entirely nonfictitious commentary that follows.

534-30-9797 felt an instant of panic. Awash in documents as he worked on his income tax, he pawed through for something with his name on it. For an awful moment, the only identity he could find in the sea of paper was that of checking account 019-238657 or mortgage number 3658. At last his eye lit upon his own name—on the TV program-guide wrapper he was using as scratch paper—and he continued, fascinated, to read his identification *in toto:* BARRY FRANK WIKSTEN, V060 00 11050 0032B0656-290310451166694, plus his address in Port Washington, New York 11050.

Wiksten, an otherwise normal

Trans World Airlines executive, had suffered a slight attack of *numerophrenia gravis*, or numbers madness, as the social critic Russell Baker named this common syndrome of the '60s, whose victims felt they were being dehumanized and turned into numbers by creeping computer technology. Later Wiksten figured out how many numerals he represented (or represented him) to business and government. He was 1473345 to the Marines; 534-30-9797 both to the Social Security Administration and to the Internal Revenue Bureau; 1935 2395 to the vital statistics division of the Department of Public Health in Seattle, where he was born; 001 279 106 7 to the American Express Company's credit-card processors; C547172 to the Department of State's passport division and 0-130173951-8007066631 to the Book-of-the-Month Club.

Some of his identities were only dimly familiar: 19-6847, his savings account; his three life insurance policies, 83 72 51, 30 053 533 and 26 814 997; his homeowner's policy HO1-73-18923; real-estate registry, 47767; title insurance, 282372LC; his lawyers' client number, 11052M; his automobile insurance policy, 970131 3881; the serial number of his Porsche, 115292; his driver's license, W0941329783 64249; and his Shell and Mobil credit cards, 877 282 384 and 831 863 420 4.

Right on the tip of his tongue, of course, were (212) 557-3904, his office phone; (516) 767-3645, his home phone; and 42 (Class 3, Type 641), his TWA pass. He also had numbers for his air travel card, his Playboy key and charge accounts at six stores. Several less active

numbers were filled with warm associations: BB/22398, his wife's birth certificate; 221, their Newton, Massachusetts, 1962 marriage license, and 56-65-101541 and 156-63-103446, the Newton birth certificates of son Eric and daughter Karen. Their second son had been born after they moved to a New York suburb, where, strange to say, registration numbers were not put on birth certificates. The poor kid started life with only a name: Kurt.

"A specter," said the social psychologist Erich Fromm, "is stalking in our midst.... It is a new specter: a completely mechanized society ... directed by computers; and in this social process, man himself is being transformed into a part of the total machine."

The transformation was being pressed vigorously by business, among others. Now the serial number, not the name, was what counted. The letter welcoming the customer to the credit plan might start out, "Dear Sir or Madam," but the important thing was the string of integers to which the recipient should "please refer in the event of further inquiry." (A Sears, Roebuck customer hovered between hilarity and despair over a letter he received from the company addressed to 141234 and bearing the salutation "Dear Preferred Customer.") The name imprinted on the "personalized" bank check became smaller and the coded account number ever larger—usually in the unwritable, mutant-looking computer version of the Arabic numerals. One New York city bank, Marine Midland Grace, aware of the alienating effect of the cybernetic hieroglyphics printed on its checks, repro-

duced a long line of the deformed characters in a newspaper advertisement and added, in parentheses, "At Marine Midland Grace we call him Harry."

But it was the Post Office and phone company that really hit the outraged citizen where he lived. The mail service announced that henceforward all addresses were to include a five-digit number that would disclose at a glance his section of the country, state, city and neighborhood—in essence, making his address all but unnecessary. Comptroller General Elmer B. Staats went even further: he proposed that town names be dropped entirely from postmarks, leaving only a zip code number to show where the letter came from. Indignant mail poured in from the rockbound coast of 04609 to the sunny shores of 92014. One magazine writer with an ear for the old tunes waxed nostalgic about such old songs as "Shuffle Off to 14202," and "37402 Choo-Choo."

Then the Bell Telephone System began replacing all geographical names with area code numbers, and exchange names—all those ORchard 6s and MArble Hill 3s—with more numbers. It was a bad day at (501) 878, formerly Black Rock, Arkansas. The faceless, and now placeless, customers rebelled. In (415), an area many people continued to call San Francisco, a group of individuals formed the Anti-Digit Dialing League, dedicated to bringing back the banished and beloved YUkons, KLondikes and VAlencias. The publicity they stirred up made the Pacific Telephone Company so nervous that it changed San Francisco to (415) months earlier than it had planned.

Protest also flared against the computer itself. One rebel published a 125-page handbook of anti-computer guerrilla tactics called *The Beast of Business*. He suggested playing "computer-card roulette"—carefully cutting, with a razor blade, three or four extra rectangular holes and returning the card to the sender (he claimed thus to have altered a magazine subscription card so that he got 23 copies of the magazine each week and a note thanking him for using the publication in his current-events class). He also advocated closing the existing holes with Scotch tape, erasing the magnetic coding on personal checks by running the code numbers under an electromagnet, and always overpaying or underpaying by a cent or two, which he said could send an unsophisticated computer into a state of hysteria.

The fact is, the wonderful machines needed no such impetus. The goofs they committed without human help were multifarious and sometimes monumental:

A Pittsburgh truck driver, after battling an appliance store for six months over erroneous past-due notices, gave in and sent a check for the amount that the store's computer said was "due immediately"—$00.00—and promptly received a thank-you note.

A Los Angeles clothing company's computer issued a check to a janitor for $5,000 in compensation for two weeks' work.

A computer set up to pick ideal marriage partners selected a brother and sister.

Three days before the primary election in which Boston's Mayor John F. Collins was running for nomination to the Senate, the mu-nicipal computer, efficiently and without instruction, prepared, addressed and mailed 30,000 delinquent sewer tax bills. The mayor lost the nomination.

An Albany, New York, hospital sent a woman patient a bill for $25 for a "ritual circumcision."

Computer mistakes could be rectified. The real danger of the cybernetic revolution, some Americans believed, lay not in the fallibility of the machine but in its omniscience. Not only was the government considering setting up a national data center where three billion "person-records" would be consolidated and computerized, but private industry was also plunging enthusiastically into the data-bank business. Life insurance companies established a firm called the Medical Information Bureau, which kept files on 11 million insurance applicants. The files contained, among other things, information on the applicants' mental condition, travels, driving record, drinking habits and even extramarital affairs. And the 2,200 credit-investigating firms of the Associated Credit Bureaus Inc. exchanged information on 100 million people who had applied for credit in department stores and elsewhere. Some of the company investigators asked prospective customers questions that seemed pretty far removed from credit, such as: "Do you have any criticism of the character or morals of any member of the family?"

One legal expert proposed that Americans be kept from becoming the victims of their own records by the creation of laws to protect their "data beings"—just as present statutes guarded their physical beings. He suggested, as a counterpart to the writ of habeas corpus—that greatest single legal safeguard to freedom—the creation of a "writ of habeas data," which would guarantee that personal information could only be released by a court order.

Meanwhile, people who couldn't lick the computer were learning to live with it, and even to exploit it. Naturally, college students were in the vanguard of this movement.

Dartmouth's pioneer time-sharing computer was employed not merely to analyze Purcell and Plato, but to play baseball games (HOME RUN ***, the computer batted out at one point. WHAT DO THE ASTERISKS MEAN?, the student asked it. APPLAUSE, said the computer). The computer was also called upon to replay the climactic Princeton football game of Dartmouth's 1962 undefeated season, and even to write letters home ("Dear Dad, This letter is being typed by a General Electric Computer. I have been very busy lately, hope this will suffice until I can find the chance to answer your letter personally. Your loving son. P.S. Send money").

For astrologers, the computer plotted propitious times for romance; for dating bureaus, it matched couples; it even made pastors more efficient by compiling profiles of their congregations. It was already possible, therefore, for a young man, with the aid and consent of a computer, to meet a girl, plot out their economic future, and marry her in a well-ordered church of their choice. Such a couple might not object at all if their first-born should be slapped at birth with a number. When they acquired a computer of their own, they might even name it Kurt.

Quite suddenly from where the
stern of the Zeppelin nested
on the ground broke out a light of
insufferable brilliancy. A
luminous gas seemed to boil out
in whirls of furious brightness
and the dirigible from the land of
One mounted with a velocity that
increased by prodigious bounds.
Within half a minute its
light was reduced from the terrific
glare of a furnace to a
radiance like that of a shooting
star. In the Valle de Rio
Infiernillo lingered a
phosphorescent mist.
"Gentlemen," quavered M.
Demetriovich, "I believe we have
on us the residual emanations of
radium. It will likely kill us.
Let us go wash it off."

T. S. STRIBLING
THE GREEN SPLOTCHES, 1927

The awesome lift-off of T. S. Stribling's radium-powered "Zeppelin" was exceeded as a spectacle by nonnuclear Apollo 8 in 1968.

lift-off

The firing of moonbound Apollo 8 on December 21, 1968, marked what rocket expert Wernher von Braun called "man's first step away from this abode to another heavenly body." The voyage was a spectacular one—69 hours from Cape Kennedy, Florida, to lunar orbit, 20 hours at an altitude of 70 miles above the lunar surface, and then the 57-hour return trip to splashdown.

The lift-off was appropriately dramatic. A solid column of flame from the five first-stage engines of the enormous Saturn V rocket lit the early morning sky, and the sound produced shock waves strong enough to register on barographs in New York, 1,000 miles away.

All of the Apollo statistics were awesome. The huge rocket engines gulped 15 tons of fuel per second and provided enough thrust to propel 500 jet fighters. The rocket and spacecraft combined were as tall as a 36-story building and weighed as much as a destroyer.

Less than 12 minutes after lift-off, Apollo 8 was orbiting the earth 118 miles up, at 17,400 miles per hour. Now a laconic exchange between astronauts Frank Borman, Jim Lovell and Bill Anders in space and Mike Collins on the ground signaled the historic moment.

COLLINS: You are go for TLI [Trans-Lunar Injection].

APOLLO: Roger, understand.

The engines fired and Apollo 8 was off to the moon.

The Astronauts

As the challenge of putting an American on the moon caught the imagination of the nation, a crew of short-haired, clean-cut young men became the unflappable heroes of the space age. These were the astronauts, hand-picked from the ranks of volunteer test pilots to risk the unknown dangers of outer space in America's three-stage approach to the moon. For the first stage, called Project Mercury, seven men were picked (one was later scrubbed due to a heart flutter) to fly alone in a series of shots that tested the ability of both men and spacecraft in suborbital and orbital flight. Mercury was followed by Project Gemini, in which two-man teams maneuvered to rendezvous and link up with other spacecraft. Then it was time for the final step: Project Apollo. At the outset of Apollo, a tragic launching-pad fire killed three astronauts and delayed the moon program by almost two years. But by the end of 1968, the astronauts were again on the move; and by decade's end the distant moon had come within what seemed easy reach. The cost: three lives and an estimated $23 billion.

MERCURY 3	MAY 5, 1961

ALAN B.
SHEPARD JR.

536 miles
15 minutes, 22 seconds

The first American to fly in space, Shepard soared 116 miles into the ionosphere aboard the Mercury capsule Freedom 7 on a brief suborbital flight that reached a speed of 5,100 miles an hour.

MERCURY 4	JULY 21, 1961

VIRGIL I.
GRISSOM

539 miles
15 minutes, 37 seconds

Gus Grissom's flight aboard Liberty Bell 7, almost identical to Shepard's, ended in near-disaster when the capsule sank after splashdown and Grissom was barely rescued from drowning.

MERCURY 6	FEBRUARY 20, 1962

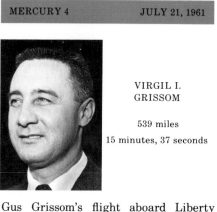

JOHN H.
GLENN JR.

81,000 miles
4 hours, 55 minutes,
23 seconds

The first American to orbit the earth, Glenn rode the 360,000-pound thrust of an Atlas booster into space before making three circuits in Friendship 7.

MERCURY 7	MAY 24, 1962

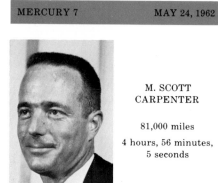

M. SCOTT
CARPENTER

81,000 miles
4 hours, 56 minutes,
5 seconds

Carpenter duplicated Glenn's feat in Aurora 7 despite constant trouble that included an overheating spacesuit, faulty instruments, misfiring rockets and splashdown 250 miles off-target.

MERCURY 8	OCTOBER 3, 1962

WALTER M.
SCHIRRA JR.

154,000 miles
9 hours, 13 minutes,
11 seconds

In a virtually perfect flight, Wally Schirra flew six orbits around the earth in Sigma 7, reaching a maximum altitude of 176 miles before splashing down only four miles from the recovery ship.

MERCURY 9	MAY 15, 1963

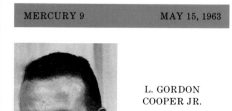

L. GORDON
COOPER JR.

583,000 miles
34 hours, 19 minutes,
49 seconds

On the last flight on the Mercury series, Gordo Cooper sent back the first TV pictures from space while also establishing a 22-orbit U.S. endurance record.

GEMINI 3   MARCH 23, 1965

VIRGIL I. GRISSOM   JOHN W. YOUNG

80,000 miles

4 hours, 53 minutes, 0 seconds

In a capsule named for an "unsinkable" Broadway heroine—a sly reference to Mercury 4—Grissom and Young flew three orbits in the first Gemini test.

GEMINI 4   JUNE 3, 1965

JAMES A. MC DIVITT   EDWARD H. WHITE II

1,610,000 miles

97 hours, 56 minutes, 11 seconds

Ed White's 20-minute spacewalk at the end of a gold-coated cable was the highlight of Gemini 4's 62-orbit journey.

GEMINI 5   AUGUST 21, 1965

L. GORDON COOPER JR.   CHARLES CONRAD JR.

3,338,000 miles

190 hours, 56 minutes, 1 second

Starting out clean-shaven and fit, Cooper and Conrad lost eight pounds each and grew stubbly beards while topping the best Russian endurance effort with a flight of eight days and 120 orbits.

GEMINI 6   DECEMBER 15, 1965

WALTER M. SCHIRRA JR.   THOMAS P. STAFFORD

450,000 miles

25 hours, 51 minutes, 24 seconds

Kept from a scheduled October launch when the Agena target rocket with which they were to dock failed to orbit, Schirra and Stafford waited for Gemini 7 before lifting off to execute an improvised plan: a 185-mile-high close-formation flight with Gemini 7.

GEMINI 7   DECEMBER 4, 1965

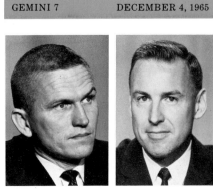

FRANK BORMAN   JAMES A. LOVELL JR.

5,717,000 miles

330 hours, 35 minutes, 13 seconds

In the 11 days before and two days after their space rendezvous with Gemini 6, Borman and Lovell logged 206 orbits —a distance equal to 12 round trips to the moon—and completed 17 experiments. One produced a photograph of Cape Kennedy from 140 miles up in which their launch pad was visible.

GEMINI 8   MARCH 16, 1966

NEIL A. ARMSTRONG   DAVID R. SCOTT

181,000 miles

10 hours, 42 minutes, 6 seconds

Six and a half hours after Armstrong and Scott lifted off, they completed the first space docking with an Agena target rocket. Minutes later, uncontrollable gyrations, caused by a runaway thruster on the capsule, forced them to undock and return to earth 60 hours early.

GEMINI 9	JUNE 3, 1966

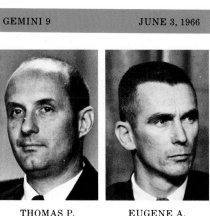

THOMAS P.
STAFFORD

EUGENE A.
CERNAN

1,256,000 miles
72 hours, 20 minutes, 56 seconds

After a balky Agena foiled Gemini 9's primary docking mission, these astronauts brilliantly executed a backup plan that included Cernan's two-hour space walk and a nearly perfect splashdown —only a mile from the recovery vessel.

GEMINI 10	JULY 18, 1966

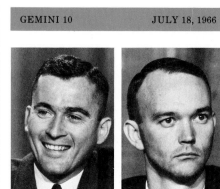

JOHN W.
YOUNG

MICHAEL
COLLINS

1,223,000 miles
70 hours, 46 minutes, 45 seconds

Gemini 10 rendezvoused with two different Agena rockets, docking with one of them. Later Mike Collins space-walked to the other to retrieve an experimental package that measured the density of micrometeorite fall in outer space.

GEMINI 11	SEPTEMBER 12, 1966

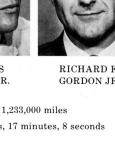

CHARLES
CONRAD JR.

RICHARD F.
GORDON JR.

1,233,000 miles
71 hours, 17 minutes, 8 seconds

Conrad and Gordon linked up with an orbiting Agena and used its power to reach a record height of 853 miles. Later, after they undocked 180 miles up, the astronauts created earthlike gravity by pinwheeling the two vehicles—linked by a 100-foot rope—around each other.

GEMINI 12	NOVEMBER 11, 1966

JAMES A.
LOVELL JR.

EDWIN E.
ALDRIN JR.

1,629,000 miles
94 hours, 34 minutes, 30 seconds

During the four-day flight of Gemini 12, the last exercise in space before Project Apollo, Buzz Aldrin was required to perform an extensive series of open-hatch activities that included simple calisthenics, photography and space walking.

APOLLO 1	JANUARY 27, 1967

1. VIRGIL I. GRISSOM
2. EDWARD H.
WHITE II
3. ROGER B.
CHAFFEE

Destroyed by
Fire

The Apollo moonshot program began tragically. During a practice countdown on the launch pad three weeks before the scheduled lift-off, the crew of Apollo 1 perished in seconds when fire flashed through their oxygen-filled cabin. The entire space program was halted until engineers had designed a safer capsule.

1. WALTER M. SCHIRRA JR.

2. DONN F. EISELE

3. R. WALTER CUNNINGHAM

4,500,000 miles

260 hours, 8 minutes, 45 seconds

Project Apollo, delayed 21 months by the Apollo 1 fire, finally began with an 11-day test that included 163 earth orbits.

1. FRANK BORMAN

2. JAMES A. LOVELL JR.

3. WILLIAM A. ANDERS

580,000 miles

147 hours, 0 minutes, 11 seconds

Launched by a Saturn V rocket's 7.5 million pounds of thrust, Apollo 8 carried men into moon orbit for the first time.

1. JAMES A. MC DIVITT

2. DAVID R. SCOTT

3. RUSSELL L. SCHWEICKART

3,926,000 miles

241 hours, 0 minutes, 53 seconds

In the first test flight of the lunar module, the moon landing vehicle successfully docked and undocked in earth orbit.

1. THOMAS P. STAFFORD

2. JOHN W. YOUNG

3. EUGENE A. CERNAN

831,000 miles

192 hours, 3 minutes, 23 seconds

The last rehearsal for the actual landing saw a lunar module named Snoopy drop to within nine miles of the moon.

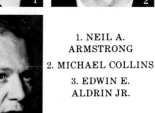

1. NEIL A. ARMSTRONG

2. MICHAEL COLLINS

3. EDWIN E. ALDRIN JR.

953,000 miles

195 hours, 18 minutes, 35 seconds

The fifth manned Apollo flight met the goal set eight years earlier by President Kennedy, when Armstrong and Aldrin left their rippled footprints on the moon July 20, 1969. After an eight-day mission, the men of the Apollo 11 project were hailed by President Nixon for having provided "the greatest week in the history of the world since the Creation."

The Pullman cars on the Pacific Railroad could not surpass the projectile vehicle in solid comfort. Besides the usual mathematical instruments, the travellers took some extra barometers, thermometers and telescopes, the Map of the Moon, three Spencer rifles and three fowling pieces, a good supply of picks, spades, handsaws and other necessary implements, plenty of clothing suitable for all temperatures, two beautiful dogs, several packages of the most useful seeds, a dozen or two of young saplings, a small cask of the best Cognac.

JULES VERNE
FROM THE EARTH TO THE MOON, 1865

Verne's cannon-fired moon projectile had room for amenities missing in the instrument-crammed cabin of "Molly Brown."

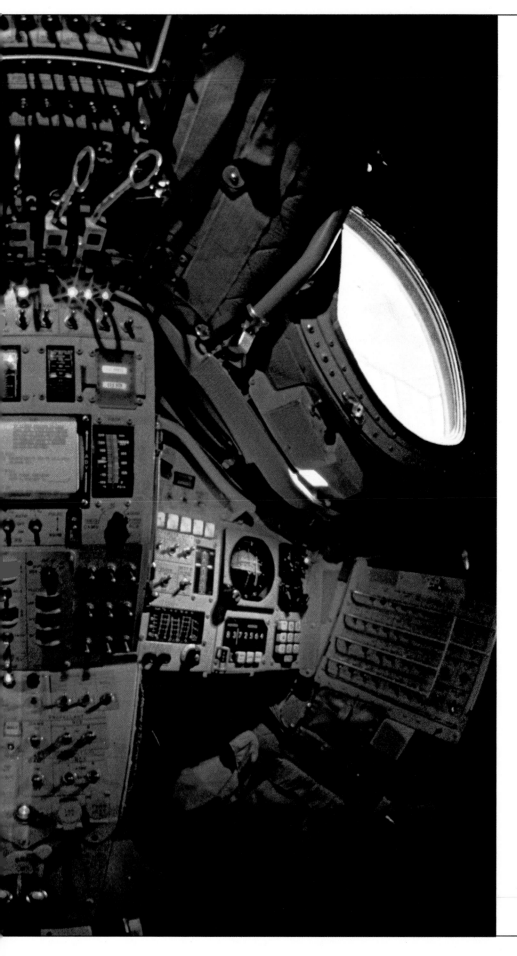

The Spacecraft

In the elaborately instrumented cabin of the Gemini capsule, "Molly Brown," astronauts Virgil "Gus" Grissom and John Young made the first two-man U.S. space flight on March 23, 1965. The array of 384 switches, knobs and dials visible in the picture at left controlled everything from the air conditioning in the spacesuits to the 32 rockets used to maneuver the spacecraft during its three-orbit journey around the earth.

Grissom praised the cabin as "a very businesslike, no-nonsense layout, and the only thing they didn't include is Muzak." (For Gemini 5, music actually was piped in.)

Gemini's sophisticated instrumentation was an outgrowth of the simpler but often unrealiable Mercury controls. Most of the Mercury astronauts were wary of the capsule's automatic controls and popularized a word, glitch, that described an unaccountable electrical malfunction, such as a warning light that suddenly flashed when no emergency existed. An exasperated John Glenn said: "Man has been piped aboard as pilot of the spacecraft. Now we can get rid of some of that automatic equipment and let man take over."

Instead, the engineers produced the highly computerized Gemini controls, and then went a step beyond for the three-man Apollo spacecraft. The vehicle that took the first men to the moon was equipped not only with elaborate backup systems, but with anti-glitch test equipment to check all of the systems in flight.

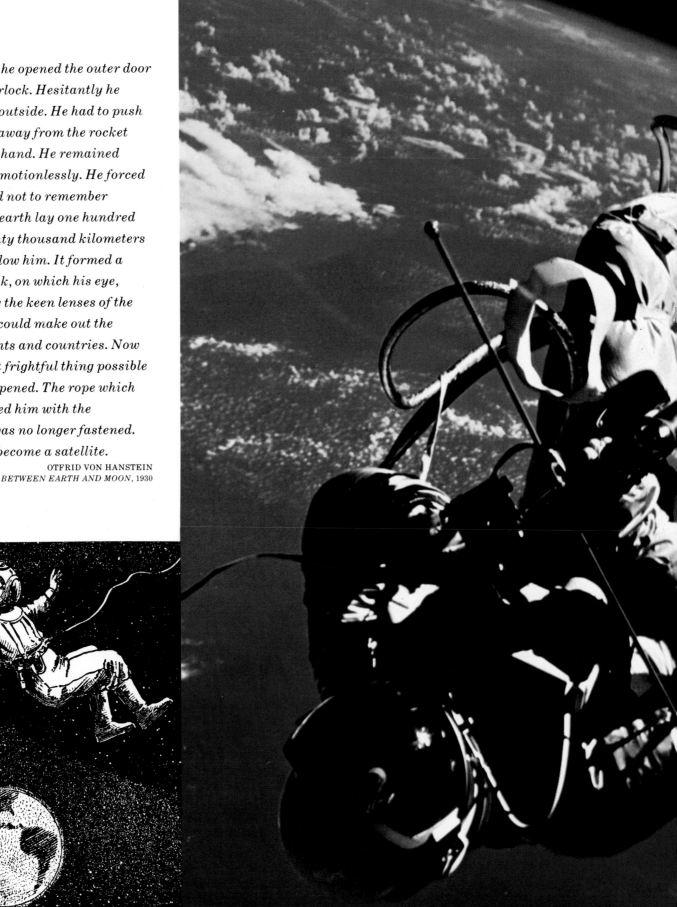

*Quickly he opened the outer door
of the airlock. Hesitantly he
stepped outside. He had to push
himself away from the rocket
with his hand. He remained
floating motionlessly. He forced
his mind not to remember
that the earth lay one hundred
and eighty thousand kilometers
down below him. It formed a
huge disk, on which his eye,
aided by the keen lenses of the
helmet, could make out the
continents and countries. Now
the most frightful thing possible
had happened. The rope which
connected him with the
rocket was no longer fastened.
He had become a satellite.*

OTFRID VON HANSTEIN
BETWEEN EARTH AND MOON, 1930

A terrified spacewalker from Otfrid Von Hanstein's 1930 space thriller was equipped much as carefree Ed White was in 1965.

276

Floating in Space

On June 3, 1965, astronaut Ed White floated out of the Gemini 4 capsule to become the first American to "walk" in space. Here is part of his conversation with capsule-bound Jim McDivitt during the historic 20-minute stroll.

WHITE: I'm looking right down and it looks like we're coming up on the coast of California. And I'm going in slow rotation to the right. There is absolutely no disorientation association.

MC DIVITT: Ed, will you please roll around. Right now we're pointing just about straight down to the ground.

WHITE: OK. The sun in space is not blinding but it's quite nice. I can sit out here and see the whole California coast.

MC DIVITT: You smeared up my windshield, you dirty dog.

WHITE: Yep.

MC DIVITT: Ed, I don't even know exactly where we are but it looks like we're about over Texas. As a matter of fact that looks like Houston below.

WHITE: We're looking right down on Houston. I'll get a picture.

MC DIVITT: They want you to come back in now.

WHITE: This is fun.

MC DIVITT: Back in. Come on.

WHITE: Hate to come back to you, but I'm coming.

MC DIVITT: You still have three and a half days to go, buddy.

WHITE: O.K. I'm on top of it right now. Aren't you going to hold my hand?

MC DIVITT: No, come on in.

WHITE: All right.

MC DIVITT: Come on. Let's get back in here before it gets dark.

WHITE: It's the saddest moment of my life.

"You behold here a Micro-Crystalline Televisor," explained Rand. "The first of it's kind ever created. Do you wish a demonstration?"

Across the ten-foot reaches of the screen there flickered wild vegetation. Much more startling was the huge beast-like shape that burst through the thicket, and stood as though posing for its portrait.

For a moment I stared at this outlandish thing. "It is unbelievable!"

"Nothing is unbelievable," he dogmatized, "when you are looking at another planet. You are viewing a typical scene on Mars."

STANTON A. COBLENTZ
MISSIONARIES FROM THE SKY, 1930

A TV view of another world, predicted by Stanton Coblentz, comes true as New Yorkers in Central Park watch the moon walk.

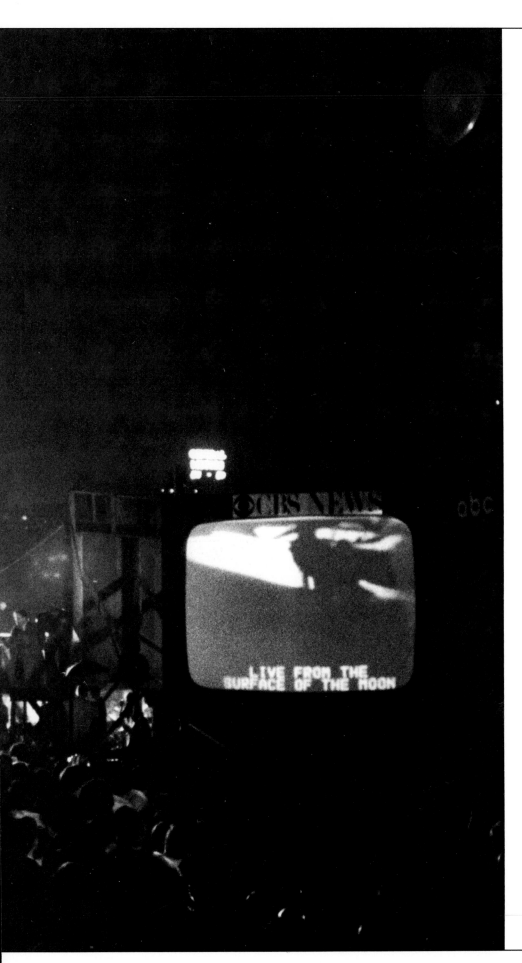

The Moon Walk

Apollo 11 blasted off for the moon at 9:32 a.m. EDT on July 16, 1969, and its mission was exactly 102 hours and 46 minutes old when astronaut Neil Armstrong, the command pilot aboard the spiderlike LM (lunar module), radioed earthward these historic words: "The Eagle has landed." Mission Control in Houston replied with ill-suppressed excitement, "We copy you on the ground. You've got a bunch of guys about to turn blue. We're breathing again. Thanks a lot."

This feeling of relief and jubilation was echoed in messages from all over the world *(overleaf)*. But almost at once, the tension began building again toward the next crucial moment of the mission, when Armstrong and astronaut Buzz Aldrin were scheduled to begin man's first physical exploration of another world.

While a third astronaut, Mike Collins, orbited the moon in the mother vehicle, Columbia, Armstrong and Aldrin got on with their complex preparations for what space scientists called EVA, Extra Vehicular Activity. At the same time, an estimated worldwide audience of 600 million prepared for a subsidiary miracle long anticipated by science-fiction writers: they would see another world, live, on television. As early as 7:30 p.m., thousands of New Yorkers began assembling in Central Park to watch the moon-walk on three huge screens set up in the Sheep Meadow. The whole world was bound together by concern for two explorers farther from home than man had ever ventured.

When all was in readiness aboard the LM, the two astronauts opened the hatch and aimed the TV camera at the steps leading down to the surface of the Sea of Tranquillity. Then from Mission Control in Houston came confirmation that all systems were go—including the television.

HOUSTON: Okay, Neil, we can see you coming down the ladder.

ARMSTRONG: I'm at the foot of the ladder. I'm going to step off the LM now. That's one small step for a man, one giant leap for mankind. The surface is fine and powdery. I can—I can pick it up loosely with my toe.

HOUSTON: Neil, this is Houston, we're copying.

ARMSTRONG: There seems to be no difficulty in moving around as we suspected. It's even perhaps easier than the simulations of one-sixth g that we performed on the ground. Okay, Buzz, we're ready to bring down the camera.

ALDRIN: I'm all ready. I think it's been all squared away and in good shape.

Twenty minutes later, Aldrin joined Armstrong on the lunar surface, and for 51 minutes the astronauts went about their carefully planned tasks, setting up scientific experiments, collecting lunar samples. At 11:47 p.m. EDT, their EVA was interrupted by word from Mission Control.

HOUSTON: Tranquillity Base, this is Houston. Could we get both of you on the camera for a minute, please? The President of the United States would like to say a few words to you.

NIXON: Neil and Buzz, I am talking to you by telephone from the Oval Room at the White House. And this certainly has to be the most historic telephone call ever made. I just can't tell you how proud we all are. For every American, this has to be the proudest day of our lives. And for people all over the world, I am sure they, too, join with Americans, in recognizing what a feat this is. Because of what you have done, the heavens have become a part of man's world.

At that moment, the mission of Apollo 11 still had some 85 hours to go before the three astronauts splashed down in the Pacific Ocean 825 miles southwest of Honolulu. In that period, there would be several more critical moments. But the performance of the men and machines had been so precise that when President Nixon signed off, millions of viewers went to bed confident of the astronauts' safe return.

Absolutely bloody marvelous.
A LONDON CLERK

Fantastically marvelous.
WIFE OF ASTRONAUT MICHAEL COLLINS

It's great to be alive on this day —hats off to America.
PRIME MINISTER BURNHAM OF GUYANA

I'd like to be an astronaut. It sounds like a pretty good job to me. Good pay and you find something new every time you go up.
A MICHIGAN BOY, AGE 12

It means nothing to me. I have no opinion about it, and I don't care.
PABLO PICASSO

The United States and Russia can do anything they want because they have the money. Poor people like us can't and that's the way the world will always be. But good luck to them.
A CHILEAN METAL WORKER

Along with this development of space, we must protect the surface of the earth. That's even more important.
CHARLES A. LINDBERGH

Congratulations and best wishes to the courageous space pilots.
PRESIDENT PODGORNY, U.S.S.R.

While we can send men to the moon, we can't get foodstuffs across town to starving folks in the teeming ghettos.
THE REVEREND JESSE JACKSON

Nothing in show business will ever top what I saw on television today.
GINA LOLLOBRIGIDA

Moon or no moon, we have to go on making cheese. After all, we can't turn the cows off.
A PHILADELPHIA CHEESE MANUFACTURER

It's something spiritual.
JACQUES LIPCHITZ

Everyone started murmuring and laughing. I wanted to stand up and sing. I felt like yelling out loud. I was really proud.
A GI IN VIETNAM

My wife, she says they're really not on the moon at all, they're just somewheres in South Jersey.
A NEW YORKER

The New York Times

LATE CITY EDITION
Weather: Rain, warm today; clear
tonight. Sunny, pleasant tomorrow.
Temp. range: today 80-66; Sunday
71-66. Temp.-Hum. Index yesterday
69. Complete U.S. report on P. 50.

VOL.CXVIII..No. 40,721   © 1969 The New York Times Company.   NEW YORK, MONDAY, JULY 21, 1969   10 CENTS

MEN WALK ON MOON

ASTRONAUTS LAND ON PLAIN; COLLECT ROCKS, PLANT FLAG

Voice From Moon: 'Eagle Has Landed'

EAGLE (the lunar module): Houston, Tranquility Base here. The Eagle has landed.

HOUSTON: Roger, Tranquility, we copy you on the ground. You've got a bunch of guys about to turn blue. We're breathing again. Thanks a lot.

TRANQUILITY BASE: Thank you.

HOUSTON: You're looking good here.

TRANQUILITY BASE: A very smooth touchdown.

HOUSTON: Eagle, you are stay for T1. [The first step in the lunar operation.] Over.

TRANQUILITY BASE: Roger. Stay for T1.

HOUSTON: Roger and we see you venting the ox.

TRANQUILITY BASE: Roger.

COLUMBIA (the command and service module): How do you read me?

HOUSTON: Columbia, he has landed Tranquility Base. Eagle is at Tranquility. I read you five by. Over.

COLUMBIA: Yes, I heard the whole thing.

HOUSTON: Well, it's a good show.

COLUMBIA: Fantastic.

TRANQUILITY BASE: I'll second that.

APOLLO CONTROL: The next major stay-no stay will be for the T2 event. That is at 21 minutes 26 seconds after initiation of power descent.

COLUMBIA: Up telemetry command reset to reacquire on high gain.

HOUSTON: Copy. Out.

APOLLO CONTROL: We have an unofficial time for that touchdown of 102 hours, 45 minutes, 42 seconds and we will update that.

HOUSTON: Eagle, you loaded R2 wrong. We want 10254.

TRANQUILITY BASE: Roger. Do you want the horizontal 55 15.2?

HOUSTON: That's affirmative.

APOLLO CONTROL: We're now less than four minutes from our next stay-no stay. It will be for one complete revolution of the command module.

One of the first things that Armstrong and Aldrin will do after getting their next stay-no stay will be to remove their helmets and gloves.

HOUSTON: Eagle, you are stay for T2. Over.

Continued on Page 4, Col. 1

VOYAGE TO THE MOON

By ARCHIBALD MacLEISH

Presence among us,

        wanderer in our skies,

dazzle of silver in our leaves and on our
waters silver,

    O

silver evasion in our farthest thought—
"the visiting moon" . . . "the glimpses of the moon" . . .

and we have touched you!

        From the first of time,
before the first of time, before the
first men tasted time, we thought of you.
You were a wonder to us, unattainable,
a longing past the reach of longing,
a light beyond our light, our lives—perhaps
a meaning to us . . .

    Now
our hands have touched you in your depth of night.

Three days and three nights we journeyed,
steered by farthest stars, climbed outward,
crossed the invisible tide-rip where the floating dust
falls one way or the other in the void between,
followed that other down, encountered
cold, faced death—unfathomable emptiness . . .

Then, the fourth day evening, we descended,
made fast, set foot at dawn upon your beaches,
sifted between our fingers your cold sand.

We stand here in the dusk, the cold, the silence . . .

and here, as at the first of time, we lift our heads.
Over us, more beautiful than the moon, a
moon, a wonder to us, unattainable,
a longing past the reach of longing,
a light beyond our light, our lives—perhaps
a meaning to us . . .

    O, a meaning!

over us on these silent beaches the bright
earth,

    presence among us

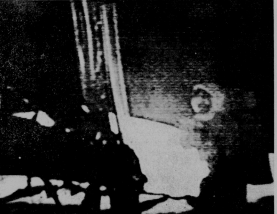

Neil A. Armstrong moves away from the leg of the landing craft after taking the first step on the surface of the moon

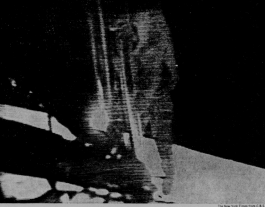

Col. Edwin E. Aldrin Jr. climbing down the ladder. The television camera was attached to a side of the lunar module.

        The New York Times from C.B.S. News

Mr. Armstrong, right, and Colonel Aldrin raise the U.S. flag. A metal rod at right angles to the mast keeps flag unfurled.

    Associated Press

A Powdery Surface Is Closely Explored

By JOHN NOBLE WILFORD
Special to The New York Times

HOUSTON, Monday, July 21—Men have landed and walked on the moon.

Two Americans, astronauts of Apollo 11, steered their fragile four-legged lunar module safely and smoothly to the historic landing yesterday at 4:17:40 P.M., Eastern daylight time.

Neil A. Armstrong, the 38-year-old civilian commander, radioed to earth and the mission control room here:

"Houston, Tranquility Base here. The Eagle has landed."

The first men to reach the moon—Mr. Armstrong and his co-pilot, Col. Edwin E. Aldrin Jr. of the Air Force—brought their ship to rest on a level, rock-strewn plain near the southwestern shore of the arid Sea of Tranquility.

About six and a half hours later, Mr. Armstrong opened the landing craft's hatch, stepped slowly down the ladder and declared as he planted the first human footprint on the lunar crust:

"That's one small step for man, one giant leap for mankind."

His first step on the moon came at 10:56:20 P.M., as a television camera outside the craft transmitted his every move to an awed and excited audience of hundreds of millions of people on earth.

Tentative Steps Test Soil

Mr. Armstrong's initial steps were tentative tests of the lunar soil's firmness and of his ability to move about easily in his bulky white spacesuit and backpacks and under the influence of lunar gravity, which is one-sixth that of the earth.

"The surface is fine and powdery," the astronaut reported. "I can pick it up loosely with my toe. It does adhere in fine layers like powdered charcoal to the sole and sides of my boots. I only go in a small fraction of an inch, maybe an eighth of an inch. But I can see the footprints of my boots in the treads in the fine sandy particles."

After 19 minutes of Mr. Armstrong's testing, Colonel Aldrin joined him outside the craft.

The two men got busy setting up another television camera out from the lunar module, planting an American flag into the ground, scooping up soil and rock samples, deploying scientific experiments and hopping and loping about in a demonstration of their lunar agility.

They found walking and working on the moon less taxing than had been forecast. Mr. Armstrong once reported he was "very comfortable."

And people back on earth found the black-and-white television pictures of the bug-shaped lunar module and the men tramping about it so sharp and clear as to seem unreal, more like a toy and toy-like figures than human beings on the most daring and far-reaching expedition thus far undertaken.

Nixon Telephones Congratulations

During one break in the astronauts' work, President Nixon congratulated them from the White House in what, he said, "certainly has to be the most historic telephone call ever made."

"Because of what you have done," the President told the astronauts, "the heavens have become a part of man's world. And as you talk to us from the Sea of Tranquility it requires us to redouble our efforts to bring peace and tranquility to earth.

"For one priceless moment in the whole history of man all the people on this earth are truly one—one in their pride in what you have done and one in our prayers that you will return safely to earth."

Mr. Armstrong replied:

"Thank you Mr. President. It's a great honor and privilege for us to be here representing not only the United States but men of peace of all nations, men with interests and a curiosity and men with a vision for the future."

Mr. Armstrong and Colonel Aldrin returned to their landing craft and closed the hatch at 1:12 A.M., 2 hours 21 minutes after opening the hatch on the moon. While the third member of the crew, Lieut. Col. Michael Collins of the Air Force, kept his orbital vigil overhead in the command ship, the two moon explorers settled down to sleep.

Outside their vehicle the astronauts had found a bleak

Continued on Pages 2, Col. 1

Today's 4-Part Issue of The Times

This morning's issue of The New York Times is divided into four parts. The first part is devoted to news of Apollo 11, and includes Editorials and letters to the Editor (Page 16). Poems on the landing on the moon appear on Page 17.

General news begins on the first page of the second part. The News Summary and Index is on the first page of the third part, which includes sports news, obituaries (Page 51) and transportation news and weather reports (Pages 50 and 52).

Financial and business news begins on the first page of the fourth part.

Following is the News Index for today's issue:

HERE MEN FROM THE PLANET EARTH

FIRST SET FOOT UPON THE MOON

JULY 1969, A.D.

WE CAME IN PEACE FOR ALL MANKIND

NEIL A. ARMSTRONG
ASTRONAUT

EDWIN E. ALDRIN, JR.
ASTRONAUT

MICHAEL COLLINS
ASTRONAUT

RICHARD NIXON
PRESIDENT, UNITED STATES OF AMERICA

A long way from home, astronaut Buzz Aldrin salutes a nylon American flag that he planted on the surface of the moon.

Acknowledgments

The editors of this book wish to thank the following persons and institutions for their assistance:

Mrs. Virginia Blacker, New York City; Paul Bonner, The Condé Nast Publications Inc., New York; Romeo Carraro, *Los Angeles Times;* Mrs. Alaine Cort, Fabergé, New York City; Ace Diamond, Diamond-Brophy Associates, Los Angeles; Harold Holden, president, Golden Rain Foundation, Seal Beach, California; Mrs. Eleanor McMillan, The Fashion Group, New York City; Steve Milgrim, Operation Match, Great Neck, New York; Sam Moskowitz, Newark, New Jersey, for his science-fiction collection; Joel Pomerantz, Grossinger's Hotel, Grossinger, New York; Martin N. Quamma, administrator, Leisure World, Seal Beach, California; Susanne Smolka, *Los Angeles Free Press;* Ray Stuart, R.R. Stuart Collection, Los Angeles.

Picture Credits

The sources for the illustrations in this book appear below. Credits for pictures from left to right are separated by semicolons, from top to bottom by dashes.

6,7—Gerry Cranham from Rapho Guillumette. 8,9—Bob Richards. 10,11—Richard Henry for Life. 12,13—Robert W. Kelley for Time. 14,15—Gordon Tenney for Life. 16,17—Frank Dandridge for Life. 18,19—Gary Winogrand. 20,21—Allan Grant for Life. 22,23—Henri Dauman for Life. 28—Walter Daran courtesy David Levine reprinted with permission from *The New York Review of Books.* Copyright © 1966 The New York Review. 30,31—Herbert Orth. 32,33—Arthur Rickerby for Life. 35—Paul Schutzer for Life. 36,37—Joe Scherschel for Life. 38,39—Copyright © 1963 James B. Mahan. 40—Arthur Rickerby for Life—Bob Gomel for Life—Ralph Morse for Life. 41—Mark Shaw for Life. 42,43—George Tames courtesy *The New York Times.* 44,45—Photographs Copyright © Jacques Lowe except bottom right Bob Gomel for Life. 46,47—Mark Shaw for Life. 48,49—Paul Schutzer for Life. 50,51—Peter Anderson from Black Star for Life; Arthur Rickerby for Life. 52—Elliott Erwitt from Magnum. 53—Charles Harbutt from Magnum. 54,55—Burt Glinn from Magnum. 57—Vernon Merritt III for Life. 58—Robert Ronge, Rochester, New York. 60,61—United Artists. 62,63—Lee Baker Johnson except upper left Steve Schapiro for Life and bottom right David Gahr for Time. 64—Bill Eppridge for Life. 65—Bill Eppridge for Life except upper left and upper right John Dominis for Life. 66,67—John Dominis for Life. 68—James Jowers from Nancy Palmer Photo Agency. 69—Jerrold N. Schatzberg. 70 through 76—Bonnie M. Freer from Photo Trends. 76,77—Moos-Hake/Greenberg from Peter Arnold. 78,79—"Kaleidospicture" by Raymundo de Larrain. 80, 81—Eugene Anthony from Black Star; B. MacLean © 1967 Bill Graham No. 75; Wes Wilson © 1966 Bill Graham No. 39; Wes Wilson © 1967 Bill Graham No. 56—Wes Wilson © 1967 Bill Graham No. 50; B. MacLean © Bill Graham No. 79; B. MacLean © 1967 Bill Graham No. 76. 82,83—©Max Waldman 1969. 84,85—Art Kane; Moos-Hake/Greenberg from Peter Arnold. 86,87—Fred W. McDarrah; Grey Villet for Life. 88,89—Pete Turner. 90,91—Copyright 1963, *The Dallas Times-Herald* and Photographer Bob Jackson, via AP Wirephoto. 93—Harry Benson. 94—Don Uhrbrock for Life. Background United Press International. 95—Office of the Sheriff, Shelby County, Tennessee. Background Joseph Louw courtesy Life. 96—Los Angeles Police Department. Background Bill Eppridge for Life. 99—© 1963 *The Chicago Sun-Times* reproduced by Courtesy of Wil-Jo Associates and Bill Mauldin. 100,101—Richard Avedon photograph for *Vogue:* Copyright © 1967 by The Condé Nast Publications Inc. 103—Howell Conant for Life. 104—Bert Stern. 105—Barry Kaplan for Life. 106—Ken Duncan. 107—Ronald Fitzgibbon from Camera Press; Richard Avedon photograph for *Vogue:* Copyright © 1969 by The Condé Nast Publications Inc. 108,109—Raymundo de Larrain. Coat by Cuddlecoat, Boots by Herbert Levine, Scarf by Saint Laurent-Rive Gauche; Raymundo de Larrain. 110—Penati photograph for *Vogue:* Copyright © 1968 by The Condé Nast Publications Inc.; James Moore—Richard Davis. 111—Richard Davis. 112—Raymundo de Larrain. 113—Charles Tracy. 114—Ken Duncan. 115—Franco Rubartelli for *Vogue:* Copyright © 1969 by The Condé Nast Publications Inc. 116 through 127—Bill Ray for Life. 128, 129—Bob Peterson for Life. 131—Micro Photo Division, Bell & Howell Co., Cleveland, Ohio. 132—Martha Holmes. 134—Henri Dauman for Life. 136,137—James H. Karales *Look* Magazine Photo © 1965.

139—Charles Moore from Black Star. 140,141—Bruce Davidson from Magnum. 142,143—Robert Phillips for Life; Francis Miller for Life. 144,145—Gordon Parks for Life; Robert W. Kelley for Life. 146-147—Henri Dauman for Life. 148, 149—Declan Haun from Black Star for Life. 150, 151—Bud Lee for Life. 152,153—Enrico Sarsini for Life. 154—Marvin Lichtner for Life. 155—Ken Regan from Camera 5. 156—Frank Dandridge for Life. 157—Sahm Doherty from Camera 5. 158,159—Charles Moore from Black Star. Background Herb Orth courtesy Liberty House No. 2. 160,161—Charles Blackwell. Background Herb Orth courtesy Liberty House No. 2. 162—Al Satterwhite from Camera 5; Fred Bauman for Life. 163—NBC; Charles Blackwell. 164,165—Oggi Products, Inc. 166,167—Arthur Schatz for Life. 169—John Dominis for Life. 170—Steve Schapiro for Life; NBC—Walter Daran. 171—Charles Moore from Black Star for Life—Milton Greene for Life; John Dominis for Life. 172—Henri Dauman for Life; United Press International—© Philippe Halsman for Life; Bill Ray for Life. 173—Vernon Merritt III for Life—Truman Moore for Life; Ken Regan from Camera 5 for Time. 174—Santi Vasalli from pix—Alfred Statler for Time; Robert W. Kelley for Life. 175—Arthur Schatz for Life; Julian Wasser—Burk Uzzle from Magnum; John Olson for Life. 176—Henry Grossman for Life—Loomis Dean for Life; Bill Eppridge for Life; David Gahr for Time. 177—Peter Polymenakos; Steve Schapiro for Life—Martha Holmes for Life. 178—Francis Miller for Life—Lee Lockwood from Black Star for Life; Bill Eppridge for Life—Wide World. 179—No Credit—Enrico Sarsini for Life; United Press International. 180—Steve Schapiro from Black Star; David Gahr; © 1969 by United Feature Syndicate, Inc.—I.C. Rapoport for Life. 181—Francis Miller for Life; Francis Miller for Life; Arthur Schatz for Life—Truman Moore for Life. 182—Steve Schapiro for Life; Enrico Sarsini for Life—© Walt Disney Productions; Henri Dauman for Life. 183—Wide World; Shel Hershorn from Black Star for Life—Alfred Eisenstaedt for Life; John Olson for Life. 184,185—Burk Uzzle from Magnum. 187—Clemens Kalischer. 188,189—Gordon Tenney for Life; John Dominis for Life. 190,191—Alfred Eisenstaedt for Life. 192,193—Burk Uzzle from Black Star for Life. 194, 195—Gordon Tenney for Life. 196,197—Yale Joel for Life. 198,199—Bruce Davidson from Magnum. 200,201—Lionel Martinez. 203—Larry Burrows for Life. 205—Larry Burrows for Life. 206,207—Ken Hamblin for *Detroit Free Press.* 208,209—Larry Burrows for Life; Ralph Crane for Life. 210—Richard Meek. 211—Wide World. 212—Courtesy of International Poster Corp. Copyright © 1968. 213—Walter Daran; No Credit—Marjorie Pickens. 214,215—Paul Conklin for Time. 216,217—David Burnett; Walter Daran—Frank Johnston for Time (2). 218,219—Flip Schulke for Life. 220,221—Walter Daran; Paul Schutzer for Life. 222—Roger Malloch from Magnum. 225—Artist Gino Beghé, New York City, © 1969 Encore Art Prints, New York City. 226,227—Mark Kauffman for Life. 229—Walter Iooss Jr. for Sports Illustrated. 230—Bob Gomel for Life; Arthur Fillmore—Jerry Cooke for Sports Illustrated; Heinz Kluetmeier for Sports Illustrated. 231—Arthur Shay for Time—James Drake for Sports Illustrated. 232,233—© 1967 by special permission of Mark McCormack for Sports Illustrated—Gerry Cranham from Rapho Guillumette for Sports Illustrated. 235—Lois Holland Calloway Inc. 236,237—Lee

Balterman. 239—Rowland Scherman for LIFE. 242—Michael Leroy courtesy *Cosmopolitan* Magazine. 243—Courtesy Compatibility Services, Inc. 244,245—Truman Moore for LIFE; Lee Balterman for LIFE. 246—Bill Ray for LIFE. 247—Arthur Schatz for LIFE. 248,249—Courtesy South Bay Club Reporter; Bill Ray for LIFE; Arthur Schatz for LIFE—Bill Ray for LIFE. 250,251—Arthur Schatz for LIFE. 252—Courtesy Grossinger Hotel. 253—Courtesy Mr. and Mrs. Charles H. Kane. 254,255—Neil A. Armstrong for NASA. 257—Magazine illustration selected from the science fiction collection of Sam Moskowitz. Illustration by Frank R. Paul from *Science-Fiction Plus* (August, 1953). 258,259—Magazine illustration selected from the science fiction collection of Sam Moskowitz. Illustration by Warwick Goble from *Pearson's Magazine* (August, 1896); Stan Wayman for LIFE. 260,261—Myra Mangan from magazine illustration selected from the science fiction collection of Sam Moskowitz. Illustration by Hans Waldemar Wessolowski from *Amazing Stories Quarterly* (Fall, 1931); Fritz Goro for LIFE. 262,263—Phil Brodatz for LIFE from magazine illustration selected from the science fiction collection of Sam Moskowitz. Illustration by Frank R. Paul from *Air Wonder Stories* (August, 1929); J.R. Eyerman for LIFE. 264,265—Magazine illustration selected from the science fiction collection of Sam Moskowitz. Illustration by Frank R. Paul from *Wonder Stories* (April, 1933); Henry Groskinsky for LIFE. 268,269—Magazine illustration selected from the science fiction collection of Sam Moskowitz. Illustration by Frank

R. Paul from *Amazing Stories* (March, 1927); NASA courtesy LIFE. 270—NASA; Don Uhrbrock for LIFE; Walter Bennett for TIME—No Credit; Walter Bennett for TIME—Wide World; Walter Bennett for TIME. 271—Ralph Morse for LIFE; Walter Bennett for TIME; Don Uhrbrock for LIFE (3)—No Credit; Don Uhrbrock for LIFE—Don Uhrbrock for LIFE (2); Walter Bennett for TIME; Don Uhrbrock for LIFE (2); Ralph Morse for LIFE. 272—Don Uhrbrock for LIFE; Ralph Morse for LIFE; Don Uhrbrock for LIFE; Ralph Morse for LIFE (2)—No Credit; Don Uhrbrock for LIFE—Ralph Morse for LIFE—Don Uhrbrock for LIFE; Ralph Morse for LIFE; Don Uhrbrock for LIFE; Ralph Morse for LIFE. 273—Walter Bennett for TIME; Ralph Morse for LIFE; Don Uhrbrock for LIFE; Ralph Morse for LIFE; NASA—Ralph Morse for LIFE (2); Don Uhrbrock for LIFE; Ralph Morse for LIFE—Ralph Morse for LIFE—Don Uhrbrock for LIFE (4)—Ralph Morse for LIFE (2). 274,275—Illustration from *From the Earth to the Moon* by Jules Verne (1865); Farrell Grehan for LIFE. 276—Magazine illustration selected from the science fiction collection of Sam Moskowitz. Illustration by Frank R. Paul from *Science Wonder Quarterly* (Fall, 1930); NASA. 278,279—Magazine illustration selected from the science fiction collection of Sam Moskowitz. Illustration by Frank R. Paul from *Amazing Stories* (November, 1930); Charles Moore for LIFE. 281—© 1969 by The New York Times Company. Reprinted by permission. 282,283—Neil A. Armstrong for NASA courtesy LIFE.

Bibliography

Bender, Marylin, *The Beautiful People.* Coward-McCann, Inc., 1967.
Bernstein, Jeremy, *The Analytical Engine.* Random House, 1964.
Breitman, George, *Malcolm X Speaks.* Grove Press, Inc., 1965.
Cleaver, Eldridge, *Soul on Ice.* Dell Publishing Co., Inc., 1968.
Didion, Joan, "The Hippie Generation." *The Saturday Evening Post,* September, 23, 1967.
Goldstein, Richard, *The Poetry of Rock.* Bantam Books, Inc., 1969.
Grissom, Virgil "Gus," *Gemini.* The Macmillan Company, 1968.
Holnquist, Anders, and Peter Marin, *The Free People.* Outerbridge & Dienstfrey, 1969.
Klagsbrun, Francine, and David C. Whitney, eds., *Assassination, Robert F. Kennedy, 1925-1968.* Cowles Education Corp., 1968.
Lewis, Richard S., *Appointment on the Moon.* The Viking Press, 1968.
McLuhan, Marshall, *The Gutenberg Galaxy: The Making of Typographic Man.* University of Toronto Press, 1962.

McLuhan, Marshall, *Understanding Media: The Extensions of Man.* McGraw-Hill Book Company, 1964.
The New York Times, The Kennedy Years. The Viking Press, Inc., 1964.
Quant, Mary, *Quant by Quant.* G. P. Putnam's Sons, 1966.
Rosenthal, Raymond, ed., *McLuhan: Pro & Con.* Funk & Wagnalls, 1968.
Schlesinger, Arthur M., Jr., *A Thousand Days.* Fawcett Publications, Inc., 1965.
Sorensen, Theodore C., *Kennedy.* Harper & Row, 1965.
Tebbel, John, *The Compact History of the American Newspaper.* Hawthorn Books, Inc., 1963.
Wolfe, Tom, Walter Kerr, Judith Crist, Emily Genauer, Maurice Dolbler, Eugenia Sheppard, Red Smith, Clementine Paddleford, *New York, New York.* The Dial Press, 1964.
Yablonsky, Lewis, *The Hippie Trip.* Western Publishing Company, Inc., 1968.

Text Credits

60—By William Hedgepeth from the July 23, 1968, issue of *Look* magazine. Copyright 1968 by Cowles Communications, Inc. 71,74—From a forthcoming book on THE HOG FARM by Hugh Romney to be published by Simon & Schuster in 1971. 130—Condensed from "Requiem for the Post" by Stewart Alsop, *Newsweek* January 20, 1969, Copyright Newsweek Inc., 1969. 133—From *The Best of Grantland Rice*, selected by Dave Camerer, Franklin Watts, Inc., 1963, p. 33; From *Out of the Red* by Red Smith, Alfred A. Knopf, 1950, p. 237; From *New York, New York*, by Clementine Paddleford et al., The Dial Press, 1964, p. 174; From *The Kandy-Kolored Tangerine-Flake Streamline Baby* by Tom Wolfe, Farrar, Straus and Giroux, 1965, p. 204. 135—Excerpts from *Understanding Media: The Extensions of Man* by Marshall McLuhan, McGraw-Hill Book Company, 1964, pp. 29, 326, 327, 328. 141—Copyright 1966, 1967 Art Buchwald. 142—"We Shall Overcome." Royalties derived from this composition are being contributed to The Freedom Movement under the trusteeship of the writers. 144—© 1963 by Martin Luther King Jr., by permission of Joan Daves. 162—Courtesy Flip Wilson and

Dick Gregory. 163—Courtesy Nipsey Russell and Jimmy Walker. 164—Courtesy Godfrey Cambridge. 210—From *Promenade*, Book and Lyrics by Maria Irene Fornes, Music by Al Carmines. 220—From the book *Letters From Vietnam*, edited by Bill Adler, Copyright © 1967 by Bill Adler. Used by permission of E.P. Dutton & Co., Inc. 235—Paul C. Marcus, Pro Sports, Inc. 258—From "In the Abyss" by H.G. Wells, *Pearson's Magazine*, August, 1896. 260—From "Seeds of Life" by John Taine, *Amazing Stories Quarterly*, Fall, 1931. 262—From "The Silent Destroyer" by Henrik Dahl Juve, *Air Wonder Stories*, August, 1929. 264—From "The Man Who Awoke" by Laurence Manning, *Wonder Stories*, April, 1933. 268—From "The Green Splotches" by T.S. Stribling, *Amazing Stories*, March, 1927. 274—From *From the Earth to the Moon* by Jules Verne, 1865, translated by Edward Roth. 276—From "Between Earth and Moon" by Otfrid Von Hanstein, *Science Wonder Quarterly*, Fall, 1930. 278—From "Missionaries from the Sky" by Stanton A. Coblentz, *Amazing Stories*, November, 1930. 281—© 1969 by The New York Times Company. Reprinted by permission.

Index

Numerals in italics indicate an illustration of the subject mentioned.